I'M HERE

To
Yuonne
Lots of Love
Bry — Sept 92

By the same author:-

Just A Touch Away
(Regency Press £4.95)

I'M HERE LISTENING

by

BRYAN GIBSON

Regency Press (London & New York) Ltd.
125 High Holborn, London WC1V 6QA

ISBN 0 7212 0892 4

Printed and bound in Great Britain by
Buckland Press Ltd., Dover, Kent.

CONTENTS

This book is dedicated to:

Every one in the spirit world and to
every one on the earth plane.

To the families of those mentioned for
their permission and help.

To my special guide Running Foot
and my spiritual family and friends.
Without their knowledge and guidance this
book could not have been written.

Thank you also to Monica, Paul, Dawn
and John for their help and support.

Bryan, 1992.

Death is nothing at all
I have only slipped away
Into the next room.
I am I, and you are you.
Whatever we were to each
Other, that we are still.

Call me by my old familiar name.
Speak to me in the easy
Way which you always used.
Put no difference into your tone;
Wear no forced air of
Solemnity or sorrow.

Laugh, as we always laughed
At the little jokes we enjoyed
Together. Play, smile, think of me.
Pray for me.
Let my name be ever
the household word that it always was.

Let it be spoken without affect,
Without the ghost of a shadow on it.
Life means all that it ever meant;
It is the same as it ever was.

There is absolutely unbroken
Continuity. What is this death
But a negligible accident?
Why should I be out of mind
Because I am out of sight?

I am but waiting for you
For an interval –
Somewhere very near,
Just around the corner.
All is well.

Canon Holland of St Paul's.

INTRODUCTION

"Listen! We really *are* listening." That's what they tell me. "We hear your thoughts, your words and your love. We just want you to know that every day and every night we *are* listening."

Suddenly, members of our family, our most treasured partners or special friends are taken away from us to begin their new life in the world of spirit. At this, our lives become very empty and loneliness and desperation take over. This is when we want our loved ones to be able to hear us and hopefully to know that they *are* there listening.

It is as if, each morning, we awake and say to them, "Good morning. I love you" and "I miss you so much", and we want our voice to be heard. With our last message each night – "God bless" – we wonder and hope that they are listening to us. Not only do we get frustrated as we wish for some sign of their presence, wanting to relate to them, hoping to have a glimpse of them or hopefully to hear their voice, we feel despair and find it so hard to understand.

When everyone is together as a complete family on earth, we accept the every-day decisions and situations as normal, but once one member leaves us for the spirit world beyond, all these problems are so much more enlarged, and we find it so hard to come to terms with. It is at the times when we talk to them of all those little things which have gone wrong that we wish they were here to help with and give words of comfort, the times when we need their help in making difficult decisions, when the children need the love and guidance we feel only they could have given, that frustration and loneliness make us call out in despair to be heard.

I would like to reassure each and every one that your loved ones are listening and trying to give you their thoughts, and hopefully direct you into making the right moves which will help and guide you onto the right pathway.

Although you may feel you cannot hear their voices, listen to the thoughts that come into your mind instinctively, that is their way of communicating with you in the hope that you will be able to understand and that you will go ahead and make the decisions which you now feel are correct, and which seem the sensible thing to do.

Because of our frustration, anger and sadness, often we are inclined to reject these thoughts, to doubt the thoughts and ideas that are coming into our minds and it is at this stage that often we are directed into the path of those who can give us the confirmation of such messages from our loved ones and relieve the doubts that have been created. As with our loved ones on earth, family and friends in the world beyond only wish to come and give their love and support which we so desperately need, and the guidance to help us to continue with our lives here on the earth plane, to help us move in the direction which will ease our pain and prevent moves which would cause us more unhappiness and problems in our lives.

As you will find hopefully, when you come to us for a sitting, your loved ones already will have been listening to you and will know of your fears and thoughts and the questions you need answering. Hopefully, you will find by the end of the sitting, that the messages relayed from your loved ones will be answers to the questions you came along intending to ask but hadn't needed to ask verbally, as your thoughts are answered through spirit. Not only will they give out their love to you, but also give help and guidance which you need so much. Many times they will recall the memories you shared together while on the earth plane, and relay messages of family and friends, speaking of the changes in their life and ensuring that they are not forgotten. They wish to let you know that they are aware of what is going on around you since they were called to the spirit world. They want you to know that they are here listening although you cannot see them or touch them, their presence is around you all the time. It is that awareness you think you can feel, yet cannot understand, that instinct when you turn around as if to answer them only to discover that they are not there but, my friends, they are there, listening to you and hoping that you will answer them by saying, "Hello".

When a child leaves us for the spirit world, it can be devastating. Perhaps the child leaves us at a very early stage of pregnancy or is taken away from the mother for reasons that, at that time are correct; it may be that the child coming into the world is stillborn or just lives for a very short time, but at whatever stage of their development it happens, not only is this devastating for the family, it is difficult for all of us to come to terms with because we feel that the child has not been given the chance to be part of our lives, to watch it grow and be happy. This is why, when a child communicates from spirit to their loved ones, people find it very hard to understand that they are capable of giving off such a lot of information about their family.

As soon as a child is created, life has begun; that life becomes aware and starts to listen during the time that the child is developing within its mother. The child is becoming in tune with its family and surroundings. It listens to our voices and the sounds around us and, when the child arrives in the world, its basic character already has been formed. It is already in tune with the sounds it has listened to during its growth. Related to as a baby, and talked to during its development within the mother, this child is not afraid.

Therefore, when this very special child has to leave us suddenly and is called into the spirit world, it already has its links and thoughts of you and, as soon as possible, given the opportunity, will wish to come down and reassure its family that it still exists and is in the world of spirit even though you cannot touch or see them. This special child will continue to grow spiritually and keep its contacts with the family here on the earth plane and to be aware of the new members of the family who arrive later. They will be watching the progress of their family and will try to give them positive thoughts to help and guide them when needed.

These special children, when they are allowed to come down to make themselves known, will always correct those receiving the message when the sitter says, "Yes. I had a child (or children)". Their child in spirit will always say, "You still have a child. We are still here with you; we are still part of the family and always wish to be talked about as if still here. They are so pleased when this happens and their younger brothers and sisters are brought up to know that they have a special brother or sister in the spirit world.

As these lovely children grow spiritually and watch and learn through us here in the earth plane, they are very aware of our lives and, as we continue to talk to them, and of them to others, it gives them great joy and happiness knowing they are still included in the family and not forgotten. Your special child or children love to hear your voices and what is happening in your lives. Because they are special children, their progress in the world of spirit is important. The knowledge they have of us here on the earth plane, they hopefully can put to use, and when they are given the chance to be able to communicate with those of us here on earth, they not only give us their love but hope to help us with guidance and also to keep the family links going until everyone, at a later date, will eventually meet up together in the spirit world.

So your special children will always be listening to you when you talk to them and send out your thoughts and love, and, when you feel strong and able to come to terms with their passing, you will be able to receive their message, letting you know they are happy and at peace with themselves, and still very much part of your lives.

Christopher

Every day is such a different day. I never can anticipate what is in store with the sittings I shall be doing and the people I shall meet.

Last month, I was very surprised when a couple who had been booked in by a friend 'phoned to ask directions, as they were travelling from Hampshire, which to me seemed quite a distance to come for a sitting, but obviously they felt the outcome would be worthwhile. They were a little car-weary when they arrived and I settled them down with a cup of coffee. We proceeded to start the sitting very quickly, as all the time I was being made very much aware of a very young child, now in the spirit world, trying to communicate and who couldn't wait to have his voice heard. After giving them the month of October, which was accepted, I was able to link them with their son who had only been in the spirit world for a few weeks. He gave me his condition of a great deal of trouble with his chest and stated that he had left very quickly. The family accepted this information very emotionally and this very special young boy followed on with the names "Christine" and "Christopher", which was his own name. He told me that his father had been married before and that Christine was his half-sister and that he also had a half-brother named Robert.

By now, Christopher was chatting very strongly. He described how his father, Graham, was self-employed and told me at about his offices. He also gave off the names of some of his work associates. Switching from one subject to another, Christopher started to talk about Thomas the Tank Engine which was his favourite. His parents told me that he spent a lot of time watching the video of Thomas the Tank, and it kept him quiet and contented.

Although up to this time Christopher had not relayed his age to me, from the way he was chattering I felt him to be about two years old, which his parents confirmed as he would be two years old in October, the next month. Christopher was still continuing to give evidence about the family which was being accepted, even talking of the funeral and the Thomas the Tank Engine wreath from his

Christopher.

parents. They, however, were still having difficulty, I felt, accepting that their special son was able to say so much, not only about himself, but also about his parents – Graham and Louise – and also their friends and situations around them. It was obvious that they felt they needed more proof of Christopher and then they asked if I could tell them what was placed inside the coffin with Christopher. I have to be honest – I was not getting anything definite to this – all I seemed to be getting from Christopher was a ring and photographs. On asking Louise and Graham if this related to anything as the image I was given of the ring circled Louise, Graham and Christopher, Graham stated that it did mean something but not to do with their question of what was placed with him in the coffin. At this stage, the telephone rang. After answering it and returning into the room, some of the tension I had felt with the sitting had gone and I felt more relaxed. As I linked up again with young Christopher, he decided it was time to give me information regarding the way he had left us for the spirit world. He started by saying that the family was on holiday abroad in Spain and that he had got an infection which had affected his lungs. He had died very quickly. Louise and Graham said this was correct and seemed pleased that he had been able to give this off so clearly and it obviously helped them, but I was still unable to give off the information asked for earlier, although I knew he would give it when he was ready.

Christopher again insisted on showing me the ring and photographs. When I asked Louise and Graham again if they could place these, all they could think of was that the photographs had just been developed which they had taken of Christopher on holiday. They had got them with them, and also Graham had just that week bought Louise a ring as a special link with Christopher, so he was correct in giving this to me, showing he was up to date with everything that had happened in the short space of time since he had arrived into the world of spirit. The photographs and ring were important but sometimes, in a sitting, misunderstandings can happen because sitters are looking for the obvious and interpretations can get confused. However, these should always be able to be cleared up and the correct explanation or meaning of the message given. After the sitting was over with Christopher's parents, they showed me the last photographs of Christopher taken in Spain and we talked a little of how I communicated with spirit. Although in some ways it had helped Louise and Graham to have this link with their son, I felt there were still doubts there, but knew their questions would be answered at the right time. With Christopher having been in spirit for such a short amount of time, everything was very emotional for them and at a later time, perhaps they will see everything a little more clearly.

A few days later, I was surprised to receive a phone call from Graham, saying he had checked up on certain things Christopher had said. Christopher had been right; when they got back and visited the grave, the only wreath left was "Thomas the Tank". Even so, Graham stated that – as a lawyer – most things to him have to be "black and white" and he still found it difficult to understand. However, as I had never met them before that day and no way could have given off so much information which they could accept as accurate, I hoped they might come to see me again at a later date to lessen his confusion.

Their very special son, Christopher, will be listening to them and when we next meet will be able to give them more positive knowledge of his progress in the world of spirit.

* * *

After this story was written, but before the book went to print, I decided to add an up-to-date item of good news in Christopher's family.

In the summer of 1991, Louise and Graham were on a visit to this part of the country and decided to arrange another sitting, to talk to their son, Christopher. This time, Louise was a few months pregnant, and Christopher was thrilled that he would soon have a brother or sister to relate to, and wanted to reassure Louise and Graham that everything would be all right. He said that it was special that the baby would have the same birthday month as his in October, and that he was watching over them all.

This week, I received a letter from his parents, enclosing a photograph I had requested for the book, with the news that their new baby had arrived on 1st October, 1991 and had been named Thomas Christopher. Both Louise and Thomas were doing very well.

Stephen

Children are so very special – not only when they are here on the earth plane – but also extra special when they have been called into the spirit world. As there is no such thing as death and the spirit continues, it is a surprise to most people left here on earth when these small, precious beings are able to come back to associate with us, not only telling us about themselves but also their family and friends. Recently a lady who had booked to see me telephoned and asked whether, as her daughter was bringing her, it would be all right for them to sit together. This was fine with me, as they were family.

When they both arrived and we proceeded to commence the sitting, I was drawn very strongly to the daughter. I was being shown a lovely little boy, who was placed in my arms and smiling. The boy told me he had suffered from a chest condition and had only been in the spirit world for a very short time. On being given this information, the young lady emotionally responded, "Yes, that's my nephew on my husband's side". Now the contact had been established, this very special young child gave me the name Paul, which was his father's name (her brother-in-law), and proceeded to give the month of September as his month of passing, which was also the month in which the sitting was being given. The young lady said, "Yes, he only left us last Friday due to an infection of the lungs". After this the young child continued to give his name – Stephen – followed by the surname "Allen" which were both accepted as correct.

By now the young Stephen was giving them very relevant information. He relayed the family names of his cousins, his mother Julie and uncles and aunts in the family.

All this time I was aware of frustration because someone else was trying to come through and communicate, but young Stephen was still there. I apologised to them, explaining that Stephen was determined to talk and didn't want to let anyone else through at the moment which they said was OK but were quite surprised at what

17

was happening. They had not even expected him at the time but now wanted him to stay and talk. After letting Stephen talk a little more about his family, older members of the family on mother's side were able to come and communicate, but not without the occasional interruption from young Stephen. He still wanted to state that he had not been buried yet and knew it would be very sad and emotional but wanted them all to be happy for him now that he was no longer suffering and was at peace. He was his parents' first child and wanted to reassure Julie and Paul that there would be other children and he would have brothers and sisters which he would always be aware of.

All through the sitting, which was very emotional, it was obvious that his aunty was meant to come that day. Stephen hoped that his family could accept his message that he is still here with them not in body, but in spirit. Even though this very special young child called Stephen had only been in the spirit world for a few days, he was determined to show that life continues. I felt very sorry that the lady who had booked the sitting had had to take a back seat, but at least she understood how important it was that Stephen's voice was heard, to show that he was listening and through spirit was able to send his thoughts and love back to each and everyone here on the earth plane.

Religion

People often question my religious belief, asking what spiritualists believe in and whether we believe in God.

Many seem very genuinely surprised when I express my belief in God and when I explain that I thank him every night for allowing me to have this wonderful gift of mediumship and ask him for guidance in using it to the best of my ability.

Some people do not regard Spiritualism as a religion, mainly listening to those of other religious orders who try unfortunately to condemn us as those who are doing the devil's work, regarding us as evil. It is sad how wrongly they are misled.

Once people are aware of Spiritualism and its value to help, without interfering in their lives, they can decide for themselves if it is right for them. However, even within our own spiritualist movement, it can be quite confusing as we have within this movement the Christian Spiritualist Church, the Two Worlds Church, the SNU churches, etc., which can be very puzzling to a newcomer in understanding how one movement (Spiritualism) can have so many different titles. I suppose, therefore, that it is not surprising that people find it complicated by this.

However, in answer to this question regarding my belief, I believe in God. I also believe, as my spirit family tells me is true, that Jesus Christ was created in bodily form and came down to express God and his work, so that we here on the earth plane could relate to God. With regard to Jesus' role here on the earth plane, we are told (and the Bible states) that Jesus gave healing and hope to those sick in body and mind, bought people back from the dead, talked to God spiritually for love and guidance and also tried to inform people of things to come. Jesus was condemned for all of this by people around him and, when Jesus finally left us for the world of spirit, came back to show us that life continues in the world beyond.

Nowadays, we as spiritualists are continuing with God's work as Jesus Christ did, helping to heal the sick through spiritual healing and showing people that those who have left us for the spirit world continue to exist in the world beyond; showing that they can come back and relate to their loved ones and friends, not only sending their love but also offering guidance to help us who are still here on the earth plane. However, even in this day and age, we are also condemned by certain religious orders and it is still no different from the way it was in the beginning.

As I am told by spirit, the Bible was created by man and written as man saw and believed things to be. Therefore it is open to question as man's interpretation of events and situations were expressed as that individual person wished to express them and write them down. So, as spirit says, a lot of the Bible is open to question as the Bible even, at times, contradicts itself, or should we say interprets things differently. This makes it very sad what many religious "fanatics" can only quote from the Bible which they believe to be correct, as "gospel", feeling it could not possibly be doubted or questioned, having no other answers apart from what is written.

As a Spiritualist, I believe in life after we have left this earth plane of ours, and now try to show people who seek this proof that life continues in the spirit world. Hopefully, we can spread the word of spirit and the work of Spiritualism so that people may be allowed to benefit from its love and guidance, whatever belief they may hold.

Every religion, if we look at it closely, has something to offer, as long as it helps people and does not dictate what must be believed. Each person should have freedom of choice to search for and find that pathway of religion which helps and comforts them. As we are sometimes aware, there are some people who cannot think for themselves and are very easily led. They have to follow like sheep because they only understand being told what to do and believe and some of these become attached to certain religious movements. Some are held to a religious belief by fear and kept in fear by leaders who scare them into believing that only they have the answers and that other beliefs are evil; that no other way of life is acceptable but their religious order. These people are then afraid to look in any other possible direction, but there are others who have an open mind and are seekers who will search for their belief, perhaps trying many different religions before they find the one which gives them the peace of mind and something to which they can relate. These people are those that many established religions are afraid of because they make their religions open to question, threatening the leaders' power and monopoly over people as those people become aware of other forms of religion which give not only more understanding but also the freedom to think and speak freely.

It is very sad when certain people within any religious movement, even within our own spiritualist movement, want only the power to manipulate others, wishing to be a so-called "tin-god". However, as often happens with power, sadly there comes with it the greed not only for more power, but also monetary benefits and dictatorship. It is a healthy sign that today so many of the younger generation are being allowed to be aware of Spiritualism and are aware of the help and comfort it conveys to those in need, not just spiritually but also in the knowledge of the wonderful gift of healing which is now so much more accepted.

I am always pleased when serving a Spiritualist church to see families with their children, as these children will be allowed to grow up not being afraid of the life beyond. Possibly, at a later stage of their development, they may choose another religious belief but at least they will have had the freedom to choose and will have known what Spiritualism is about.

Through many generations, in different walks of life and different countries, people believe in their God; perhaps not as we see our image or interpretation of God, but nonetheless it is the same God. Whether their image is perhaps an icon, a figurehead, even a stone or the sun, that is not important. What is important is the belief in God, that we are all part of God and all loved by God. Whatever we do with our lives at this material stage of life here on the earth plane, we are given freedom of choice in what to believe and how to lead our lives and should use that freedom thoughtfully. Hopefully, when we all reach the spirit world, we will understand more and put our earth experiences to a useful purpose. Also, as our loved ones and friends now in the spirit world, come and guide those here on the earth plane, a more peaceful and understanding future may be possible.

Laughter With And From Spirit

Situations which occur when working with spirit often bring a smile to our faces, but there is also the laughter which spirit shares with us about the things they see happening in our lives and they are laughing in the spirit world with us at these times as they would have done when here on the earth plane. They can still joke and pull our legs. I feel that spirit would like some of these shared with other people, so I include what I call the fun side of my work as a medium and the laughter it has created.

I was demonstrating at Ashby Country Club. This was to me another new venture with my spirit work and I was a little unsure of what to expect. When first approached, I had told the owners that as long as it was organised as an evening of mediumship and not as a variety act so that people knew what to expect, I was more than willing to appear. I was not disappointed as to me the evening showed that life continued in the spirit world. The setting of Ashby Hall is beautiful; it has a secluded position and lawns, trees and lake are kept as natural as possible, together with the wildlife. The whole setting was just perfect in its peacefulness. Inside, it was stately too. The atmosphere was right; I felt relaxed and at home and it seemed that the night would go well. At the beginning of the evening, the first few messages had been linked up and passed on to the families involved. The joining of the two worlds had begun and everything was folding nicely into place. I really love it when laughter is created by those in the spirit world and this evening was to be no exception.

On approaching a group of four people, I turned to the lady at the end who accepted evidence of an aunt in spirit and other information, but it was when her mother in spirit decided to announce herself that things began to buzz. As the four people sitting together seemed to be in some way related, all were being included in the messages. After this lovely mum in spirit had given information about herself and family, and I was about to move on to others, she said suddenly, "Mention the magazines they have got".

On hearing this message, they all began to laugh and automatically I was then told to say that Mum knew all about them and I was shown a picture of the magazine. At that point, I told the rest of the audience that I wasn't going to give them a detailed description but that they would have to use their imagination, which produced a lot of laughter. Then, without waiting, I was given the next message to relay to her daughter about the Ann Summers parties which made everyone laugh. The daughter replied, "Yes – I've just booked another one", to which her mother's response was, "I know, and if I could, I'd send an order down too" and followed with a further comment that she enjoyed watching them and joked about the things that were on sale and available in the book. She related all the fun she had watching the people at the party trying on everything, all the underwear, etc. and this produced so much laughter that it took a little time for everyone to settle down again.

This lovely lady in spirit had shown that she still maintained her wonderful sense of humour in the world in which she now lived and wanted her family to know that it never changed even though she was no longer on earth. After this, this special lady continued to pull the legs of the other members of the family there. As she was about to leave, she said to me, "Say Shirley" to her daughter, who responded with, "That's my name", so Shirley's mother in spirit had not only confirmed I was speaking to the right person, but shown those present that evening that spirit is full of laughter, that life continues, and that those in spirit are still aware of our lives here on earth.

This fun part of the evening and the laughter helped to relax everyone and the remainder of the evening certainly flowed. Because of such happy vibrations surrounding us, spirit certainly responded and I feel that many of those there that night went home happier and also a little more knowledgeable about the world of spirit. They also saw the ease with which spirit people can communicate when the atmosphere is right and the people present open-minded and not afraid to accept their messages, nor afraid to confirm the identity of the speakers.

The following night, I was booked to give an evening demonstration at Harris Street Spiritualist Church, where I always enjoy working not only because of its friendly atmosphere, but the people who attend the church are so enjoyable to link up with. The evening once again began very positively. Information from spirit was being accepted and all the spirit connections were coming through with their usual love and laughter. Suddenly, during one message a friendly cat appeared in the church (a real one, not a spirit cat) and started fussing around some of the people. Suddenly it decided to miaow which made everybody laugh, and as quick as a flash spirit responded and I found myself saying, "Tell it if it stays it will probably get a message". Through the laughing, I said to the audience, "If I start miaowing, I'll have to translate to you all" but with this the cat obviously got the message and flew out of the door as if to say, "No way!"

Once again, spirit showed that every being, including animals, are part of the spirit world and should also be made a part of spirit life. Although later in the service the cat reappeared, this time it decided to remain silent and just wandered around. To me, this was another of those special nights when we can all join in the laughter, hopefully helping those that are still unsure of spirit to realise that there is nothing to be afraid of, and by creating laughter in the churches, spirit hopefully show that it is not sadness, but lots of fun.

Even when we are giving private sittings, unexpected situations can sometimes happen. Recently, two young ladies arrived for a sitting accompanied by two very young children, one a boy of about two and a half and a little girl of no more than about eight months old. I tried to explain that it might be difficult if they became noisy as it is inclined to distract my concentration, but we decided to go ahead and see what happened.

The sitting was being recorded and it all began very well. The young boy just sat there open-eyed and never uttered a word. So also was the baby until about three quarters of the way through the sitting, when Mother asked if I would mind if she fed her. To this, I automatically quipped, "Of course not! I was once a nurse, so there is not much I haven't seen before." Obviously I had realised she was going to breast-feed the baby. At this, both ladies laughed and so the mother then proceeded to feed the baby, trying to save some embarrassment by placing the baby's cuddly toy near the baby so as not to expose too much, while all the time the recorder continued not only with the messages on the tape but the slurping of the baby feeding until the end of the sitting, so this should have made interesting listening. Not only does this emphasize that everything is natural, it also showed the ease which the mother felt with me as a medium and although some may find this a "tall story", it certainly did happen as told.

As a medium, I myself can make the odd "boob" and embarrass myself in front of a gathering and this happened recently when I was, appearing at a Civic Centre with three other mediums in aid of a charity. There were over three hundred people attending and I was the last demonstrator. Everything was going very well although, from the stage, it was a little difficult to see the audience clearly due to the lighting. Coming to what I thought was three ladies, I stated that I wished to talk to the lady with a certain coloured jumper on, to which I got no response. The lady sitting alongside put her hand up saying, "Do you mean me?". I was adamant, "Sorry, no. I want to talk to the lady with the long hair and coloured jumper. At this stage, everyone started to laugh and a voice said, "Do you mean me? I'm no lady." It was a young man who from my vantage point looked just like the girls he was sitting with.

However, after my attempts at apologising which he accepted with good humour it seemed that in the end the message was not meant for him but the lady behind. Anyway, it made everyone laugh and hopefully showed people that we are just ordinary human beings and no-one is perfect.

After the demonstration, there was a raffle and the ticket I picked out was – yes, the young man's. When he came to receive his prize, he said jokingly, "See, I've got stubble'" which the audience enjoyed and everything was accepted in the good humour which had prevailed all through the evening. Next time, perhaps I should wear glasses when doing a large demonstration.

Anton

It is only recently that a sitter asked me how I decided on the people to include in my books. To be quite honest, since I first began writing about my spiritual work and the people now involved in my life, I had not queried it before, as to me it had all happened naturally. It seemed that the special people in the world of spirit should be talked about and it was not that I chose them but that those now in the spirit world who so wished allowed their stories to be told. Those of us here on the earth plane can be helped to understand and come to terms with the loss of those whom we know who may have left for the spirit world in a similar way.

A sitting took place to link Anton with his family. When it had finished, I was aware that I had to ask their permission to include Anton, as spirit felt that it would help those who might have lost, or will lose someone in a similar way, and thus help them to understand. Although no-one can possibly take away the grief and loneliness we feel at such a time, it helps to know our loved ones are able to show that they are at peace in the spirit world and that they continue to watch over us and are still aware of us and listen to our voices when we talk about them and to them.

On an evening in September, 1991, I had a booking for four people named Frank, Rohma, Andrea and Nikki. I had no further information about them and did not know if they were family or just friends sitting together. However, when they arrived, only the three ladies appeared. They apologised for the gentleman called Frank not being with them, but said he was unsure of coming and also unsure of his feelings at that time. Looking at the ladies, it was obvious that they were family and they confirmed that they were mother and daughters. As usual, they were given a drink of coffee and made to feel at home. I then proceeded to explain to them how I worked and what they might hope to receive.

At the very beginning, the first spirit contact was not family but a very close friend of one of the daughters, who said her passing was due to cancer and that she had been young when she left for the

Anton.

spirit world. She gave her name as Alison, saying that she grew up with the family and, much to their surprise, talked of memories and the children they now had, and caused quite a lot of laughter with some of her remarks. As the family said, "We hoped she would come through and talk to us and we haven't been disappointed". Then Alison decided to take a rest and a gentleman called "Derek" wanted to have his voice heard, saying he was an uncle. At the same time, I was also relating to another voice – this time a lady, who also stated that she had had cancer and was a friend of Rhoma's. She gave her name as June which was accepted as correct by Rhoma, and more information was given by June to establish her identity and friendship. All the time these lovely people in spirit were communicating, I was very aware that someone else, very special, was waiting to make themself heard. On asking the spirit voice to give me a link, I was told to give the month of February as a passing month. At the same time, I had a strong feeling of a very positive communicator trying to link with me. The spirit person then followed with the information that he had been in the spirit world for only a few months, telling me that his passing had been very sudden and that he was quite young. I looked at Rhoma and said, "He says that you are his mother". All three ladies gasped emotionally and replied, "Yes. That's right." Responding to this, the young man started talking very quickly and quite excitedly, stating that he passed very quickly and that it was not through an illness. Although, at this stage, he seemed to be holding back a little, I knew it would all come through naturally when he wanted me to know. I began to get the sound of a name which, at first, sounded like "Anthony" which was quickly altered to "Anton" and the family responded, "Yes. That is him", adding that his age was twenty-three. At this stage, Anton became more positive about the way he had left for the spirit world, and that it had happened through his own doing. He confirmed that his life had been very mixed up, especially regarding a relationship. It had altered his life and he could not come to terms with everything. Anton then proceeded to give me trouble with my chest and I was finding it difficult to breathe, at the same time showing me his car, and I became aware of exhaust fumes. Once I had understood it, I was able to relate to the family that Anton had taken his own life by exhaust fumes. Rhoma confirmed this as correct and, once more, a lot of emotion flowed.

Anton explained to them how he felt and that now he was at last at peace with himself. He understood that, although they still could not understand or accept what he had done, he wanted to reassure them that he had intended to leave for the spirit world and, at the time, knew it was the right thing to do. He had planned it and it was not a spur of the moment decision, which his mother seemed to understand and said, "I thought that". Anton continued giving off lots of information regarding his sister, Andrea, and her family and of Ian, his brother-in-law, saying that he was self-employed, and talking of their two children (his niece and nephew.) He said that his niece had just started school that week and commented on her school uniform which made Andrea smile. Anton then directed his attention to Nikki, his other sister, and talked about her husband and their two girls, one of whom had also started school the same week. Anton mentioned his father, Frank, who he knew was having difficulty in accepting his passing and was sorry he had not been able to come. He said he wished Frank would talk more about him instead of keeping his emotions to himself and commented on his father's self-employment. Anton then went on to talk of his mother's work as a doctor's receptionist in the next village and that he was with her often at work, which made Rhoma smile. Anton's cousin, Chris, was also mentioned, with whom he got on very well. At one stage they had worked together, or talked of it. The sitting was now flowing and Anton was coming through very clearly, determined to give off as much information as possible.

The conversation moved on to talk of his parents' recent holiday in America and Anton was very sorry that he had spoilt it. It appeared that this was when Anton decided to leave for the spirit world, as he knew no-one would be around. Turning to his mother, Anton mentioned that his bedroom was still the same but he still did not like the curtains. Rhoma stated he never did as they were too flowery for him, and she promised to change them for him. Anton kept showing me a poster, a large one which had been taken down, at which his sister said, "Oh, that's the one I got him of Whitney Houston, who he liked" and they promised to put it up again. He continued to talk of his room and how his mother would sit and talk to him, and mentioned that his mother was now using his Hi-Fi which pleased him. At this, his mother said, "That's the message I've been waiting for. No-one knows about this, and I just wish he would show me how to work the ruddy thing, then I promise I will play his Whitney Houston records!" Anton said this would make him happy too. He also mentioned a motor bike and that it had now gone. Rhoma said that was something else she had hoped would be talked about, as Anton had spent many hours lovingly restoring the bike, only to have it stolen from his girlfriend's home, and at the time had been very upset about it.

Anton relayed still more messages and information, briefly mentioning the name "Lisa", to which the family responded, "We thought he would", although Anton gave me no follow-up message about her.

Before the sitting came to a close, Anton sent his love to all his family, once more reassuring them that he was at peace with himself and not alone in spirit. He had met up with the older members of the family and, of course, he had Alison and June to talk to. They also wished to say, "Goodbye" and promised to keep an eye on Anton for them.

I asked the family if they wished to ask me anything but their reply was, "Thank you, we have received much more than we had hoped for, especially the confirmation about the Hi-Fi and the motor bike, which Rhoma said before she came was what would leave her in no doubt that it could only be Anton, and that he is continuing in the spirit world and listening to us here on earth".

Rhoma showed me Anton's photograph then and kindly said I could keep it, and it is now placed with many others in the room which I call my "Rogues' Gallery". I like that because when I link up with spirit, I do not always get an image of the person I am communicating with. I relate to their personality and voice, which I find a positive proof of a person in spirit as, unlike images, personalities do not change.

At this stage, I knew I had to ask Anton's family for permission to include this special young man in the book. Rhoma said happily, "Yes, we would like that, as it hopefully will help others in a similar situation to us" and it is also nice that Anton can still be part of this material world and the memory will always be there for Anton's family and friends. To, me, it seemed Anton was a very lively, sensitive young man, who could not cope with life here on the earth plane, but who had now found peace in the world of spirit where he will continue to grow spiritually, always aware of his family and friends here on earth, and will wait until eventually everyone joins him at a later date. Anton will continue to send down his love and spiritual strength to his family when needed and will also be aware of any changes in the family and new members who join it.

A few days after this sitting with Anton's family, I received a lovely letter from Rhoma, thanking me for the sitting and the help and comfort they had received.

Telephone
(0400) 48480

THE OLD FARMHOUSE
SCOTTS HILL
FULBECK
GRANTHAM
LINCS.
NG32 3LB

Tuesday. 10th Sept. 1991.

Dear Bryan,

I felt I wanted to write to you and thank you for a lovely evening last Thursday with my daughters Nikki & Andrea. We came home feeling so much happier than we have for a long time. I now know for sure Anton is with us (the family) & it is a very lovely & comforting feeling. I was 99% sure there is a life after death but now all three of us are 100% convinced. You told us so many personal things about Anton that noone else would find important but to us it made us feel so much closer to him. I personally couldn't or wouldn't accept the fact that he would never come home again, but now I know he is with me and I can talk to him. I've put his poster of Whitney Houston in his bedroom I have been playing her music for him. I feel so much calmer since I saw you and more able to cope with the grief. I haven't changed his bedroom curtains yet, but I will soon !!!

It was a wonderful experience to be in your company - you have a marvellous gift. I am sure I am not the first of your "customers" to feel as I do & I hope we can see you again in the future. I even feel I can perhaps cope with Christmas now, knowing Anton will be around. It will be hard but with the help of my lovely family, and my family & friends in the spirit world, we'll get through it.

Keep up your good work, it is so rewarding giving such comfort to so many people.

Heartfelt thanks from Nikki, Andrea and myself, we hope to see you again

Very best wishes,

Rhona

Jennings.

Olivier

With the work we do, it is often difficult not to become involved and emotionally affected by the people who come into our lives. Often we realise there is little help we can give apart from love and comfort and perhaps preparing a person for their life in the world of spirit. We can demonstrate that their family or friends who are already in the spirit world can come down to talk to them, and show them that life continues after we have left this, our material plane.

Two months ago, I received a telephone call from a lady requesting healing for her son. He had been attending a children's hospital in Sheffield over the last three years for the treatment of cancer. When she contacted me, the hospital had had to say that unfortunately no further treatment could be given. Olivier, her ten-year old son, had leukaemia and the family were looking for every available possibility of help for this, their very special son. My name and telephone number had been passed on to them from someone who was aware of my work, in the hope that young Olivier could receive help from spiritual healing which would, at the least, give him a fighting chance.

An appointment was arranged for the following Sunday morning at 11.30 am. When Olivier arrived with his parents, Michael and Christiane, I explained to them how spiritual healing works in its many different ways. We try to ease the pain and make the person more positive about coping with their illness and to give them the strength to battle on.

So, with love from spirit and my healing guide, Kuros, we proceeded to give Olivier healing, hoping that it would give him the chance to overcome his illness and enable them to continue with his life on the earth plane. As I was giving healing to this young man who, during the previous three years, had smiled through so much pain and discomfort, I was made aware of an older man standing beside me, telling me that he and everyone in spirit were sending their love and healing thoughts to his grandson. I told Christiane her father was helping me, and that, although he had not been in the

Olivier.

spirit world long, he wanted Christiane to know that he was there helping Olivier. She accepted this emotionally. Apart from bringing Olivier to see me, his parents had no knowledge about Spiritualism, so were startled but pleased to know of her father's presence and seemed to wish to know more. Therefore, I asked this lovely gentleman to tell me a little more about his grandson. I was told that the young boy had a good drawing ability and had drawings around the house, which his grandad liked. This seemed to comfort the family, knowing that he was around and watching over them, as the older man had been very close to Olivier. The healing over, we discussed ways in which spirit work, and I offered them a contact number for their local Spiritualist church and its healing group, as the more available channels of help for healing, the better. They left with copies of *Psychic News* also, as I felt reading them might enable them to understand a little more of the work we do. They knew they would be welcome to bring Olivier again if they wished but, in any case, special thoughts would go out to him every night when I joined Running Foot and my other guides as well as to his family. When I went to speak at Spiritualist churches, I told them about Olivier and they put his name on their healing list too, so many thoughts and prayers went out for this young man.

As Christiane felt Olivier had received benefit from the first visit, a further appointment was made for Sunday, 23rd December, but on the previous Friday I received a call from Christiane saying that he was less well and might not be able to come that weekend. I said I would send out extra healing for him but would be available should he prove well enough to come, even if it was Christmas Day.

I was annoyed with myself after hanging up, realising that I knew neither their surname nor their telephone number, let alone where they lived. I decided that, as Christiane had promised to ring me again before Sunday, I would offer to visit Olivier if he could not come to me.

On the Sunday morning, 23rd December, at around 9.00 am, the telephone rang. It was Christiane. She just said, "I had to let you know that Olivier has left us peacefully in his sleep and is now free from his pain". I talked to her for a while. Her father wanted her to know that he had met Olivier who was now with him and that he would look after the boy from now on. Christiane asked to see me in the New Year in the hope of hearing further from her father and hopefully from Olivier. His parents felt they wanted to try to understand how their son's life would continue in his new world.

To me, it was very sad to lose someone so special and so young, especially just before Christmas. I also felt frustrated with myself because I had not been able to help more at this tragic time. It is comforting, though, to know that Olivier is now in the spirit world with his grandfather where he will be able to grow spiritually and progress, able to come down and unite with his family on the earth plane and to help many others who may need strength in coming to terms with their illness.

Two months later, when Olivier's family made their promised visit to see me, it was a very cold, snowy day. This time, Christiane and Michael brought with them Natalie, his older sister. Almost immediately, I became aware of Olivier's presence. It appeared he could not wait to get started. His first message was to send his love, to say he was all right and that his grandfather was with him. Olivier talked of the presents he had never been able to open. There was one Christiane and Michael did not know what to do about which was presenting a problem, but Olivier said he wanted it given to his friend, which they agreed to do.

This settled, Olivier talked to them of being met by his grandfather and said his journey from the earth plane into the spirit world had been peaceful. He joked about his hair and wanted them to know that it had grown again. He said he didn't look so fat as when he had been taking the drugs.

As he talked to his parents, Olivier commented on the changes that had been going on since he left, talking about building changes the plans for which had just been drawn up, and said they had altered the position of the doors on the plan, which surprised his father very much. Talking to his mother, he said she was now going back to work and was hoping to take a course. Christiane confirmed this, to which Olivier responded that she should not worry, as everything would work out all right. Looking at Michael, Olivier said that he knew his father was unsure about changes he was considering making in his self-employment, but they were the right moves to make. Young Olivier then chatted about friends and family, naming his friends Richard and Julian particularly, and then turned his attention to his sister, Natalie. He mentioned some trouble with her leg, which they confirmed, and said she used to go horse-riding and he encouraged her to take this up again.

He also commented on Natalie's ability with music. He then

decided to stir things up a bit by talking about the disagreement in progress about Natalie and her mother about Natalie learning to type. He felt Natalie should at least give it a try, to keep her mother happy. He talked about Natalie's fourteenth birthday which was coming up and told me she had won a battle with the family over her hair. "Yes", said Natalie, "I'm having it permed next week".

Olivier continued with other personal information which they could all accept. He persuaded his father to continue with plans they had for installing a fish-pond in the garden and talked about his books and drawings. He knew which one his mother had just framed and hung, which really pleased his parents. Even his cockerel, George, got a mention.

Olivier then decided to talk about his grandma who was supposed to be visiting Montreal in Canada but was reluctant to make the planned visit. He said that both he and Grandad felt she should go.

At last, Olivier went quiet. He decided that now his other grandmother, his father's mother in spirit, should come through and say, "Hello" to Michael. This grandmother had left for the spirit world before Oliver had been born, but he had now met her too.

Michael's mother stated that her name was Kathleen and gave details of her passing and age. She wanted to reassure Michael that she was at peace and had joined Christiane's father and had met her grandson. She said they would both look after him for them.

It was now time to end the sitting, but hopefully there will be many more talks with Olivier and his family. This young boy now has a special place in everyone's heart. I hope that now I can also be included as having a part in Olivier's life, along with his family and friends.

What Is A Medium

People have many different, strange interpretations of the meaning of being a medium.

Some people see us as a link-line with those who have left us for the spirit world. We are the messengers, people who can tune in to their loved ones and pass on love between family and friends, as well as direction and guidance from people who were relied upon and trusted when they were on the earth plane, people whose help and understanding are still needed by those they have left behind.

Certain people see us as the mediator, one who can point them in a helpful direction by logical advice supplied by those in the spirit world, rather than having to rely on advice which may be biased from those emotionally involved in the situations here on earth.

Some regard a medium as a counsellor, to whom they can turn for help in sorting out problems of a personal, emotional, or perhaps financial nature. When tension and fear mask the view of the way ahead, they feel that spirit can offer direction towards finding the correct pathway.

Unfortunately, there are some who see a medium as a person who will tell them their fortunes. They only want to hear of nice things to come, relationships created for them, or wins on the pools or bingo. So many desire money to come their way, to be able to create a life to look forward to without the problems and hassles of everyday life.

Having this very wonderful, special gift of mediumship, can sometimes be very frustrating. If our gift is not used or interpreted properly, it can itself create problems for those who come to see us, not only by giving them false hope and security, but by depending wrongly on spirit and becoming reliant on the medium. It is not only sad, but wrong, when people stop trying to work things out for themselves. No-one should have to rely on a medium to run their lives.

However, we can give positive help and guidance. This is why I always try to explain to people what being a medium is, and the work we are here to do. I compare it to other forms of psychic work and explain how it works as well as what they can hope to expect. However, as far as decisions are concerned, I always stress that they are the ones responsible for making decisions in their lives, not the medium.

With my work as a medium, perhaps I am a little selfish, for I prefer to be a spiritual medium and only work with and talk with those who are now in the world of spirit. When I am relating to the person having the sitting, I know then that the messages are coming from those in the spirit world who know and understand the sitter, offering words and advice acceptable to the sitter in a way they can understand. If I, as the medium, were to try to alter the interpretation, it might not relate to the sitter or confuse them; also, the spirit communicator would not feel confident working through me and might decide to "call it a day" as with us here on earth. Like us, they too have freedom of choice, and I believe have to like the medium and know that their messages will be passed on as accurately as possible. Otherwise there is no point in doing this wonderful work.

In working as a medium, It is sometimes easy to give off messages in the hope that they will fit, or to tell the receiver that they will find the meaning, or that someone in the family will be able to understand it. To me, this is not right. If the message is vague, then it is up to the medium to ask the spirit communicator to give more positive help. I understand from my spirit family that, if the medium has been given a message relating to either past or present, then the sitter should be able to accept it. Otherwise, with a little more help from spirit, it should be sorted out there and then. In a sitting, the sitter and the medium are equally important. Some people have very good memories of the past and can accept information easily. Others need their memories jogged, with more help from spirit. It can be helpful to give a sitting to a family group with varying age-groups, as usually at least one of them can recall things from the past and confirm the spirit connections.

Unfortunately, some sitters come along with only one thing in mind and are really disinterested in the past, just wanting to deal with the present and what is to come. This can sometimes create a barrier and cause a lot of hard work for the medium. Often, in such a situation, the spirit communicator will make the sitter wait right to the end of the sitting before answering their questions. Before that, if the medium is working properly with spirit, the communicator will relate messages which should be accepted by the sitter, convincing the sitter of the identity of the spirit communicator, recognising that they would have known them when they were on the earth plane. Those people who think mediumship is just sitting down and giving off messages should be made more aware of the special work of mediums and come to understand how it is used and the way in which it works. Nowadays, no-one should be in the dark about spirit or feel afraid of its gifts. Sadly, some mediums cannot be bothered to explain about relating to spirit and feel secretive about it, as if the gift belongs only to a select few. Some fear that, if they tell other people too much about it, others may become spiritually developed and then they could be less in demand as a medium or spiritual adviser.

I am sure most people realise that being a medium is something you cannot demand to be. Mediumship is a natural ability, a gift that everyone is capable of developing, but not everyone can at present put it to its correct use which is hopefully to benefit and help each and everyone here on the earth plane. Many people who are aware of this gift are afraid of it.

Firstly they do not understand it. Sometimes, because of their family background or religious dogma, they are confused and cannot cope with it. They do not have the strength to come to terms with it and are held back from using it, so they remain in a confused wilderness until eventually spirit directs them into the light and help will be given.

Others who have the gift of spirit, sometimes use it very unwisely and try to impress people by giving off dramatic messages, even death. Very often, because they do not know how to interpret, they cause trouble and distress to sitters. Of course, this merits publicity which does not help the spiritualist movement since it can turn people against spiritual awareness, having only heard a distorted story. Fortunately, however, there are many who always use their gift wisely, looking into ways to channel this special gift to the best advantage of both sitters and communicators. Many develop their gift through the work of the Spiritualist churches or through a development circle led by a spiritually experienced medium who guides and helps them to use their gift.

Some, like myself, are lucky, being plunged into spiritual awareness, and using the gift without the books or teaching, as the gift is so strong it is developed through past and present experience. You cannot get the gift from a book. Books may help many to understand about spirit and its workings, but spirit is a natural force and comes from the heart. You have to feel it – to feel the experiences of those in spirit – as well as your own experience of life, and bring them into perspective. By a combination of these two, a medium can interpret what is given and pass correct messages to those here on earth who need love and guidance as well as knowledge from those in spirit. We are all individuals. People cannot be put into boxes as different types of person. As individuals, mediums can hopefully understand what is needed and put their gift into practice when a person visits us for help and guidance.

With all the demands, pressures and problems of being a working medium, I think it remains the most wonderful experience in life – not only being in two worlds, but receiving all the love, help and comfort that spirit gives to us all still here on the earth plane. They reassure us that life continues and that those who have gone on before us will meet us one day when our time on earth is complete. No matter how long life, with all its ups and downs, proves to be, it is being part of that life which is important and what we leave behind as a mark of our having been here. No-one can ever take away our love or our memories and these continue in the world beyond. Those in the spirit world listen in to us; down here, we are trying to listen in to them.

As spirit always remind me, life here on earth is material. You can go out and buy a piece of furniture, replace something that has been broken or lost, but you cannot replace a friend or loved one in the same way. Here on earth, everyone is a special person and should be treated as such.

Darren

In my first book, *Life Beyond the Storm*, I wrote about Darren, a young man who, due to a hanging incident, left us in July, 1987, the day before his nineteenth birthday. Darren's mother, Diana, and his sister, Amanda, visited me shortly after his passing.

As Darren was a very lively and outgoing character, he was great fun to work with whenever his family came for a sitting, not only talking about his own past, but about situations which had occurred within the family since their last visit. As Diana gradually came to terms with the loss of her only son, she realised that Darren was always around and that, when she talked to him, he listened and tried to make contact with her. Whenever Diana visited a Spiritualist church, he always tried to communicate.

By this time, Diana herself became more interested in Spiritualism and decided to join a local Spiritualist church, where after a while she became a member. Over a period of time, she joined the development circle and began developing her own spiritual awareness until she herself was able to link with spirit. Soon she found herself taking a more active part in the circle as her gift developed and also on the church platform. Before Diana knew it, she was being approached by people wanting private sittings, which she now enjoys and accepts bookings for churches further afield.

I know Diana will do very well. Not only is she a very sensitive and genuine person, but, through the loss of her son, she has gained extra strength. She also is another special person and will herself now be helping those in a similar situation to come to terms with their loss/of loved ones.

Looking back at the first time Diana met me and my guide, Running Foot, we wondered whether it had ever occurred to her that she would be linking up and doing similar work herself. She and I have remained friends since 1987, not only when we meet up at spiritual churches, but I regard Diana and Darren and their family as part of our family. Whenever we get the chance, Diana comes over

Darren.

for coffee and a chat, but mind you nowadays it's nearly always about spirit, and we learn from each other.

Although it is always sad to lose someone so young to spirit, like Darren whose life was apparently about to begin, there is comfort available for us. Through Darren, Diana is now a voice for spirit and I know it will bring her much joy and laughter and keep her in closer union with Darren in spirit.

Paul And Family

More and more of my work now seems related to my ability to communicate strongly with young people who have left us for the spirit world. They have often left quickly and dramatically, and their families who are left behind have to come to terms with their passing, suffering very painful emotion and frustration. These very special children always wish to come through and communicate with their families and friends, reassuring them of their love and the fact that they are now at peace with themselves. They also show that life continues, not in the bodily form as we know it, but as a very positive, lively spirit-person who continues to watch over them, letting them know that they are aware of what is happening in their lives here on the earth plane, including fears and troubles, and trying to reassure loved ones with their love and maybe a little guidance.

One such special person was a young man called Paul. His family came to visit me shortly after Paul's passing, when he left suddenly for the spirit world on 31st October, 1990, due to a motor cycle accident, at the very young age of seventeen years.

David and Jean, Paul's parents, and his sister, Dawn, came to see me. It was obvious from the very outset of the sitting that Paul was going to be a very strong, positive communicator. He came through very clearly. He said the accident had happened on the first day of his new job as a trainee carpenter. He had been so looking forward to this job and gave the family positive details of the accident including talk of the tractor and trailer involved in the accident. He assured them that it was all very sudden and he had not suffered.

Paul then decided it was time to give me information about his family. He said his father, David, worked at the Post Office and told me about his uniform. Mum, he said, worked at Boots where she was in charge. Paul's parents accepted this as correct. His sister, Dawn, then became the subject of the conversation and she smiled and agreed when Paul announced that she had just got a new boyfriend. He then reeled off names and explained where these people fitted in the family, and recalled his many friends. Paul was a

Paul.

very popular local boy, and referred to his friends with his usual sense of humour and occasional colourful language. This made his family laugh. "That's just our Paul", they said. "He hasn't changed."

As the sitting progressed, Paul kept reassuring the family that he was now all right and that, because his passing was so sudden, he left without any pain or distress. He had accepted his transition into the new world where he now lived and wished his family to know that it had all been due to an accident and that he had not been speeding.

While the sitting was being recorded, Paul gave details of family birthdays and went on to talk about his bedroom, giving descriptions of items in the room, which David and Jean were able to confirm. At one stage, Paul became very persistent in showing me his glasses. When I asked the family if Paul wore them, Jean replied, "Yes". Paul then wanted me to take this a step further as he wanted to confirm that he was wearing them at the time of the accident. On asking the family if it made sense to them, Jean answered that there had been a question about his glasses, as the police had asked whether he had been wearing them when he left home that morning, and his mother had said he had. It was typical of Paul to reassure Jean that she was correct and that there was no question to answer.

After relating to the family for over an hour, Paul was still coming through as strongly as ever. He told his mother that he had met up with Grandad and that he was all right.

Paul still had plenty of chatter left in him but I was beginning to feel a little tired as the energy being used was really powerful. Paul was obviously aware of this and said to me that he felt his presence had been felt and that his family had accepted that it was their Paul and knew that this was only the beginning of many more chats with them at later dates.

Although Jean, David and Dawn seemed pleased to have the special reunion with Paul, I knew and understood that there was no way it could replace Paul being there with them in the body. It may, however, have helped in that they could now accept Paul was all right and that he can hear them when they talk to him not only of their love for him, but of the every-day family conversations and situations.

Once Paul had said, "Goodbye" and sent his love once more, and the sitting was over, we all continued to talk about how I relate to spirit and how I saw Paul. As I told his family, I do not always get an image of the person. It was Paul's voice that I related to and his personality. This is important: to me as you can make an image fit, but not a personality; that never changes and Paul will always be Paul with his cheeky grin and outgoing personality.

Jean and David asked if I would like a photograph of Paul to add to my large collection of special people who I now know in the world of spirit and a week later, the promised photograph of Paul arrived, delivered by Paul's father, David. David stayed for a cup of tea and a chat and, as we talked, he told me that they had played back the tape and studied it. Things which they couldn't accept at the time and couldn't relate to, they realised now fitted into place and slotted together. David asked if they could all come again to see me and we arranged that they should come back for another sitting in a while. Lots of things can happen in six months and, knowing Paul, he will hopefully be able to tell them of what has happened in their lives since their first visit.

* * *

During April, 1991, Paul's family came back to talk to him here and Paul didn't disappoint them. He came through with his usual mixture of laughter and help. He confirmed that he hadn't missed out on what had been happening and what was going on with his family and friends.

Now, when someone who knows his family, or a friend of theirs comes for a sitting, you can depend upon Paul connecting up and asking them to pass on a message to them.

Paul And Friends

About a week after the first visit from Paul's parents, I received a telephone call from a young man who asked if he could book a sitting for two people. They had lost someone close very recently, so I arranged for them to come the following Saturday evening which was the one evening I had kept free and was hoping to have to myself.

When Saturday came around, the two young men arrived on their motor bikes. At this stage, I was still unaware of who they wanted to hear from. On introducing themselves, Chris, who had made the booking, said, "I'm sorry, but my mate, Mick, couldn't come, so is it all right for Dale to take his place?" I had no objections as two people had been booked in, so it made no difference to me. On sitting down, the boys asked if it would be all right to record it. Everything was set up and I explained to them how I worked and what they might expect to hear.

On opening up, the first link I received from spirit was the month of October and asked them if they could accept this month connected with a recent passing. Both Chris and Dale said "Yes". To this, the spirit voice followed on with their age and the name of Paul and told me that I was talking to his mates and wanted me to tell them that he was pleased that they had come to see him. Paul then started to "take the mickey" and began to swear at them which made them both grin and relax, as Paul understood that they were nervous and a little wary of what to expect. Paul talked to them of the way the accident had happened and of his passing into the spirit world. Paul mentioned his motorbike to Chris which was the same type as his own had been and said that Chris should now be learning to drive a car, as it would be better for him. As confirmation, Paul told Chris that he was still working at the food factory and it was now about time he made a change and did something better and more positive. At this, Paul showed me an RAF uniform. On asking Chris if he was thinking of joining the RAF, Chris nodded and said it had cropped up recently and he was still thinking about it. Paul promptly said, "Tell Chris it's a good idea." He wanted to encourage him to take it a step further. Now Paul decided to talk of Chris's girlfriend, saying that he didn't think Chris was ready to settle down yet and encouraging Chris to take his time about things.

Now it was Dale's turn. Chris talked to Dale about his job as an apprentice mechanic, saying Dale attended college one day each week and that Paul was keeping his eye on this. Paul told Dale he knew his friend was having a few problems with his motor bike and Dale agreed. Paul then talked to Dale about a relationship which he wanted, which made him very sad and frustrated at times, reassuring him that there was someone to come into his life before long who would make him much happier. Paul also told me that Dale had celebrated his seventeenth birthday in August and he would not miss out on Dale's eighteenth next August, when they would have a good "booze up".

All this time, Paul continued to recall the memories they shared, times of drinking lager and smoking the "cigs" which had been a large part of their recent time when Paul was here in the body, and rambling on about the good times at Cadwell Park with the motor bike racing, and referring to the girls that had been part of his life.

Paul thanked them for going to visit his mum and dad and helping them. He was very pleased that so many people had attended his funeral and knew of the wreath from all his friends. He continued to give off lots of information about his time with them all and commented that some of the crowd were talking of having a holiday abroad the following year but could not make up their minds as to the destination. Paul wanted them to know that he would be there with them and joked that it would not cost him anything. He mentioned to Dale his recent visit to Peterborough and talked of his friend's recent holiday in Portugal, which surprised them. He mentioned the name "Daniel" and said he knew of the trouble which had been caused, ending in a "punch-up" and that it was all finished with now.

Paul said he thought he ought to let them know he had met up with Trevor, another of their friends in spirit who had also left through a motor bike accident the year before, and that he had company now. At this point, Paul wished to pass on a message to Mick who he knew was working in Sheffield and disliking all the travelling, saying he could see Mick changing his job for the better.

At last, it was time for Paul to say, "Goodbye". He reminded his friends that he would have a drink with them all on New Year's Eve as he still liked to be involved in their conversations.

The sitting finished, the boys stated that they were now going to see Paul's mum and dad, to let them hear the tape, and that they were pleased to know that Paul is now happy and OK.

Dale said, as he was leaving, "I feel much happier now. Paul has made me more positive about my future. He always helped me and would talk to me about my problems when he was here. Although we were both the same age, Paul always took charge and seemed to have the right answers".

Several times since Paul's passing, people whom Paul would have known have come to me for sittings. He always pops through to say "Hello", as happened recently when a young lady named Lorraine who worked for the GPO visited me. So strong is Paul's bond with his family that he always wants them to know that he is still around and listening to them.

Fox-Hunting

Most of us, I hope, have a special spot in our lives for the animal kingdom, even those of us who mask our true feelings for fear of what others may think, or to protect our image. All of us feel guilty when we see animals suffering, especially when we have perhaps caused some of it ourselves. Quite often, when I am out driving and see a dead animal on the road, whether a cat, rabbit, hedgehog or bird, I send out my thoughts and hope that its passing was quick and that it is now at peace in the freedom of the spirit world. Where animals are killed by animals for survival, I accept that this is a natural force and is nature's way of controlling their lives and survival. However, I cannot accept people killing these animals to satisfy their own pleasure or for what they term as sport. I do feel that one day these sad people will regret their involvement in these unnatural habits and hopefully will be able to revert to what Nature was really intended to be here on the earth plane, with our enjoyment of these creatures and being able to understand them better.

With regard to people who hunt for pleasure, a very strange incident happened to me one Boxing Day in December, 1986, at the very early stages of my becoming spiritually aware. That Christmas, I had invited Harry, a close friend of mine from Herne Bay, to stay at the house. His wife, Grace, had passed away a few weeks earlier after a very long battle with cancer. We had all been very close friends for over twenty years and kept in touch, visiting each other whenever possible.

Apparently, it was traditional for the local hunt to go through the village each Boxing Day although I had been unaware of this during my two previous Christmases at the farm.

This Boxing Day, however, at about midday, I put on my wellies and for some reason was pottering about in the yard, when I heard the sound of traffic going by followed by the sound of horses trotting along. I walked down the drive and the approach to the road, to be joined by Harry carrying his camera. Without any warning, and

Fox-Hunting, Boxing Day, 1986.

totally unaware of what was to happen next, I found myself shouting at the people on horse-back, in no mean words telling them that it was a pity they had nothing better to do than to go out chasing and catching defenceless creatures, and that they should be chased themselves. It appears that I was quite abusive and that my language was a choice ripe! Although many just ignored me, I do recall one rather well-educated lady responding with her very own colourful language, and my response was to say I hoped she fell off her horse in no uncertain terms. By this time apparently, poor Harry who had been standing with me had disappeared into the house, totally taken aback with my attitude, never having seen me behave in such a way in all the years he had known me. As the last stragglers were slowly going by, I then began to feel aware of what had happened. I could feel myself shaking and felt really sick as I realised that that had definitely not been me, and that for that period I had allowed a strong spirit person to come through and express all their hate and disgust at something they obviously felt very strongly about when they had lived on the earth plane.

When I went, rather sheepishly, back into the house, a rather subdued Harry said, "Bryan, I don't know what all that was about. It was as if I was standing with a complete stranger. You were definitely not Bryan – I couldn't believe it of you". Harry was not a spiritually aware person and knew very little of my new-found spiritual awareness. It took quite a lot of explaining as I didn't want to frighten Harry, as he would think he had come to stay with a real weirdo. I did not want to unsettle him; he had gone through enough emotion and really needed this break to come to terms with the loss of Grace. Thankfully, Harry did understand and it also made him a little aware of spirit, as he will often phone me up and has also read my previous book. Ever since that Boxing Day, I feel I have to give my point of view on how I feel about this (to me) very horrible so-called sport of fox-hunting. I find I have become more open about my opinions on all blood sports. When I do talk to people about it, I am more controlled with my vocabulary although unafraid to express my dislike, even though to some people it is a family tradition or just fun to chase helpless animals.

It is important that we are allowed to express our opinions as to how we see it and how we feel about the protection of Nature and its creatures.

With our work, it is not only important that we can show people that their loved ones are able to communicate from spirit, but also to show that our animals and pets who leave us for the spirit world can also come down and relate to us as when they were here on the earth plane. Whether a pet, or perhaps some animal which we protected, helped and comforted on our material plane, these animals hold a special place in our hearts. They are just as much part of life as we human beings are. It is important that their life continues to exist in the spirit world and that they too are remembered.

Very often during a sitting, people are united with a special pet who wishes to confirm their existence now that they have left the earth plane and arrived in spirit. It may be a cat, dog, bird or other animal important to the sitter and whom they miss. Often I will be made aware of this special pet by seeing it sitting by its owner as it would have done while here in the family, or, as with cats, often sitting on the person's lap purring. Once we have accepted the link with the spirit animal, it will often confirm details of such things as its breed, colour, markings and whether it had any special features or habits. More often than not, it will give its name, its character and confirms the way it left for the spirit world, whether in an accident or through old age. Sometimes it had to be taken to the vet's due to illness with perhaps a terminal growth or loss of abilities or unable to walk any more and had to be "put to sleep". In these cases, they always want to reassure the person that it was the correct thing to do as it stopped them from suffering further.

Although many people just think of them as "dumb animals" here on the earth plane, these animals have memories and – surprising to many people – can relate their life which they experienced here on earth. I admit some people are inclined to look at me a little strangely when it happens, and I bring their pet to relate to them, especially when I say to them, "It's saying this to me" and wagging its tail and smiling at me. However, if we are honest, we can admit that animals do portray expressions such as smiling and talking.

It is very funny when I go to a person in the audience during a demonstration and bring their pet through to them. Like us, when they are taken into the spirit world, they are free, no longer needing cages to contain them or protect them from other animals. It makes me smile as I see some of the audience looking around to see if, like me, they can see the budgie or parrot flying round the room. Usually, this bird who is now trying to communicate, will state its colouring and whether it talked or just sat in it, cage and cheeped. In one instance at a public demonstration, a budgie came through to a lady in the audience and gave his name as George. The audience was amused when the lady stated that it was her mother's budgie and that she had named it George after her son-in-law whom she did not like, and had called the bird "George" just to annoy him.

Often these special pets want their owners to know that they are aware other pets have taken their place, remarking on their temperaments and knowing that they can never be replaced, but all parts of their owners' lives.

More Animals In Spirit – "Brownlow"

During the seven years I have lived on this farm, there have always been cows brought in for the winter and kept in the crew yard. For some strange reason, I became involved with looking after them as a favour to Tom, the farmer, even though until then I had never in my life had any real connections with farm animals, especially cows, so it was certainly a new experience for me. However, I must admit it seemed completely natural, as if I had done all this before. Perhaps I had in a previous existence, but I felt that a lot of the help and my feeling of ease with these beautiful, but large, animals was through my wonderful guide and friend Running Foot who would chant to them. To my surprise, they would respond and always seemed calm and never nervous of my being around them.

Over the years, the cows often came back until they were old enough to have calves and then they would be transferred to the dairy farm, so I got to know some of them very well. Each winter we would have a reunion and I knew that, as soon as they heard my voice, they would respond.

One winter was a particularly sad one. That year it seemed some of the younger cows had inherited a virus which was very difficult to either contain or cure and it was very frustrating to see these beautiful creatures slowly leave us for the spirit world. I would spend many hours trying to give them spiritual healing and would often stay with them in the crew yard, talking to them and trying to comfort them until they finally left for spirit, as I hated the thought of these poor creatures lying there alone, and having no-one with them to reassure them. I just wanted them to know that they were not alone and that we did care for them. Most people would regard them just as "cows" but to me each one was special and hopefully their transition into the spirit world was peaceful. Out of all the cows I came into contact with, there was one who was very special to me. I first got to know her as a calf and she was the only brown and white one among the herd. I decided to name her "Brownlow" and she was always much more gentle and affectionate than the others. It

Brownlow.

seemed that we had a special bond and understanding. As Brownlow grew bigger, she remained just as soft and affectionate, even after her summer spells in the meadow. Eventually, it was Brownlow's turn to have her own calf which was also brown and white. Both Brownlow and her calf were brought back to the crew yard in the November and housed with a few other cows who had not calved that year. This time, although pleased to see me, Brownlow didn't seem her usual self. To me, Brownlow seemed unwell and not eating like the others, as if she was afraid and would wait until the others had had their share of the food, so I would always try to give her food separately. I spoke to the farmer about this but not a lot of notice was taken and I felt he should know if anything was seriously wrong. To me, Brownlow and her son were becoming weaker and I eventually took it on myself to separate them off by themselves, hoping that they would have some peace and not be bothered by the other cows which Brownlow seemed to be nervous about. Unfortunately all this was in vain. Both Brownlow and her son were becoming weaker and she was not able to produce enough milk to nourish her son. The farmer said that nothing could be done and said it would be useless getting the vet but decided that the calf should be bottle fed. As all of this happened during Christmas week, and I was going to be home for Christmas Day and Boxing Day, I was asked if I would look after them. I tried with all the help I could get from spirit to help these two very special animals. Brownlow had difficulty in even standing up, so I asked spirit to please give them the strength to recover. At every opportunity I would be out in the crew yard, spending time with Brownlow, talking to them and sitting cradling her head. It may sound strange to some, but I knew that Brownlow understood what I was trying to do and she would look at me with those beautiful eyes, as if to say "thank you". Brownlow's son was now unable to stand and just laid beside her. Although he was trying to suck from the bottle, it was slow and sometimes difficult. On Boxing Day, I was sitting, nursing the calf's head, as I tried to feed it from the bottle, with Brownlow lying alongside, when the calf gave one big sigh and, with the bottle still in its mouth, peacefully left at last for the spirit world. It was one of the saddest moments. I can remember sitting feeling so helpless and so annoyed that I had not fought harder to get them help sooner, as I stayed with Brownlow reassuring her that her son was now at peace and no longer suffering. I am sure she understood and I even felt that

Brownlow could understand my feeling of hopelessness and that I could only do as much as I could, as they were not my animals and I had no voice in their rearing, as to many, my knowledge of these beautiful animals would be nil.

By now, Brownlow was each day becoming weaker and it was as if she had herself given up her right to live. She just lay there and I knew it was just a matter of time before she too would be in the spirit world, once more reunited with her son. At this late stage, the farmer eventually did get someone to come and humanely put Brownlow out of her discomfort so that she could now be at peace.

To me, this very beautiful animal and her son had suffered unnecessarily and I only wish I had been in the position to have spoken out and done more for them. However to some farmers (but not all) they are just cows for raising and selling as a living for them and their lives count as nothing more than money-value To me, and to many like me, each one is important and we want them to be kept from suffering and treated with love and understanding. I hope the little I have been able to share of my love with these beautiful creatures has shown that they are loved and thought of as well as human beings, that they have known they were not alone, for what little help and comfort we can give them in their very short and sometimes sad lives here on earth is to me very important.

Gert And Daisy

At the present time in my life, the pets I have are my special cat called Poppy and a tankful of goldfish, but up to December, 1990, they had to share the place with two other special pets – Gert and Daisy, two lovely brown hens who, in their earlier days, were some of the many hens and bantams which roamed the farm. However, Gert and Daisy outlived all the others by more than two years. They were special because they were such characters and became part of our family. They were always at the door every morning waiting for the plate of cat food, very often sneaking up on Poppy and pinching hers also, and another treat was for them to be allowed in the hallway to sit on the old mat, where they would often sit alongside Poppy in perfect harmony, apart from giving her the occasional peck.

Although Gert and Daisy were no longer producing eggs, they regularly went through the motions and sat on the nest each day hoping. By this time, both Gert and Daisy were developing their own personalities; they were always together just like sisters, although Daisy appeared to be the more dominant and appeared to be the leader. They always followed either Poppy or myself around the farm, and it was just like taking a dog for a walk. The people who used to come for sittings got used to seeing them in the house and laughed about them. Some, I think, found it unhygeinic, as occasionally they made the odd "whoopsie" on their mat. I didn't mind cleaning it up, but I suppose you did have to be careful where you trod!

One morning I was very sad to find that Gertie had died in her sleep in the nest-box, looking quite at peace. I suppose I was pleased that her death had been natural and that she had had quite a good life for a hen, but now sadly Daisy was on her own. Gradually becoming more dominant, she maintained a now closer bond with Poppy and it was as if they understood each other and continued to follow us around at every opportunity. As usual, each morning and evening, she expected her ration of cat food which she now had to share only with Poppy. Much to the amusement of people watching, Daisy followed Poppy around the farm with her wings flapping as she tried to keep up with Poppy who teased her, and occasionally if Poppy got too bold with her, Daisy would give her a peck. Now, whenever the door was open, Daisy would appear and place herself on the mat in the hall, as if to say, "This is my little bit of property". Mind you, Daisy wasn't too particular at times as to where she left her mark, but I must admit that on the whole she was quite clean for a hen. Sometimes, when people visited and had to pass her, they were not always very amused, but Daisy never gave way, but just sat there. As Daisy had now become one of the characters of our home and I regarded her as part of the family, people would often ask about her and if she was still around. She always gave the appearance of looking like a sprightly, young hen even when she was quite old and it was hard to accept that one day she would leave us. The first signs I had of Daisy's deterioration was when she began to lose her sense of direction and I became aware of her difficulty in seeing. One night, I arrived home to find Daisy sitting right in the middle of the drive, obviously unable to find her way to the shed where she spent the nights. Picking her up, I placed her in her box in the surroundings she was familiar with.

The next morning, Daisy had not arrived on the door-step, so I took her food to the shed and placed it in front of her, as it was obvious that she had now become totally blind and could not eat without my assistance. I sat and pondered on what was the best way to help her so that she did not suffer, whether to let Daisy live and continue to try to feed her, or whether this would be wrong. Seeking spirit's help and guidance, I was made aware that this would not be natural for Daisy and, after a couple of days of putting off the decision, I very reluctantly asked the farmer if he would kindly put Daisy out of her distress and prevent any more suffering for her, which I felt was what spirit had given me the positive thought to do.

It was very sad to lose Daisy, as she had given me a lot of laughter and was part of our family, but I knew that she was now at peace and would be alongside Gertie where they would both be free to roam in the spirit world. They are both very often in my thoughts and I have seen them in the house. Very often, they will come into the hall as they did before, walk around and go out again, as if to say "Thanks". They are still part of our lives.

All animals, whether wild, farm or domesticated animals, are part of life, and when we look after them stay around and come back to reassure us that their life here on the earth plane was not wasted. If treated with love and kindness, they will always, in their own way, give us back the love we all shared.

Daisy and Poppy.

Relating

Often sittings can make me feel very frustrated. Many times, I have been known to say, "That's it! I'm giving it up. I am not going to work spiritually any more." I am pleased to say, though, that this doesn't last very long and by the time the next sitter has arrived for a successful sitting, it is all forgotten and, once more, I am feeling positive again.

Hopefully, by showing examples of sittings with frustrating situations, it might help those who come to see us for sittings to understand how important it is to respond to the messages and the information given off by the medium and its interpretation. This can so often be misunderstood, especially as it often refers to events and situations way back in the past which perhaps the sitter may have put to the back of their minds for many reasons. Sometimes, people only seem to want to concentrate on present-day situations, feeling the past is not important, but it is important to the way a medium works.

Recently, a young man called Ian, who was in his early twenties, booked for a sitting. He didn't appear nervous, as many people are, but I nonetheless explained to Ian how I worked and what he might expect. I began to record the sitting and my opening words were that I was being shown a lovely little child in spirit, a little girl who stated that she had left at a very early stage of her development. I felt that this could possibly have been a miscarriage, but, on giving this information to Ian, he said he could not understand it, nor relate to it at all. The spirit communicator was very strong and asked me to repeat the message, but Ian remained adamant that there was no connection with him and stated that he didn't know of anyone it could relate to. I was feeling very frustrated about this message and it seemed to make me hesitant with the sitting, so, to ease the situation, spirit changed the subject and spoke of Ian's change of work and of the test he had coming up with the outcome of possibly working abroad, which Ian confirmed as being correct, and he was pleased with this information. I continued to talk of his family, stating that he still lived with them in the council house which once again he accepted as being correct. I was still feeling hesitant and felt I was still only half communicating, as I was still aware of this young person trying to relate, and I was gradually becoming blocked out and now finding it difficult to relate. On explaining this to Ian, and giving him the reasons why they were being difficult in spirit, Ian replied, "I am not surprised. I didn't think you would find it easy". However, I still did not think I should give up and decided to battle on and try to get the confirmation of my spirit voice. After edging about for another fifteen minutes or so, I was gradually given a much more positive response and, on asking Ian if he could understand a young man in his early twenties who had left for the spirit world very suddenly, rather dramatically, only a short while before, Ian replied, "Yes. That's my brother." Now that I had this connection, everything started to flow. Ian's brother relayed his problem which he had had when on the earth plane with drink and drugs, and spoke of his very chequered and complicated life, and stated that his passing was his own doing.

Ian said, "Yes. He took his own life". Although his brother referred to it as a kind of accident, he followed on with his name, Des, and continued by talking of his friends whom Ian knew and situations connected with them. He told Ian that he was now at peace and happy in spirit.

Once more, I was given the message of a child in spirit. On asking Ian if Des had a child in spirit, he replied no, but then added, "When I was a teenager myself, my girlfriend was pregnant and it was terminated. To be honest, I had not thought about it any more, so didn't relate it to me", so the mystery of the lovely child in spirit had at last been sorted out, as she only wanted the connection with her father.

To me, in the end, it had been worthwhile to battle on with the sitting and I admitted to Ian that I had been very tempted to end the session at the beginning. However, as the frustration from spirit had been so strong, I had hoped that they would help me to sort it all out, and they had. It also taught me not to doubt my spirit voices and to work at getting the messages through, however difficult and regardless of the amount of time it takes. It is easy to relate to present-day events and often much more difficult to relate to things from the past which are not brought to mind until people have had a chance to think about everything.

I do not like to say to people, "Take it with you and think about it", or state that they may find out what is meant at a later time, as often mediums are inclined to do, as the messages given are for the sitter and, as the medium, I should be able to place it or explain the meaning of the message. Vagueness of messages worries me and, since I often stress this fact to sitters, people will often write or telephone me to give me the confirmation that the message or name did mean something and has been understood by someone else in the family.

As long as I can use my gift to the best of my ability and it helps those who need the help, I am glad, be it in communicating with loved ones in spirit or giving guidance to put people on the correct pathway.

* * *

Another example of a frustrating sitting which got off to a bad start occurred a few days later. This time, two ladies arrived for an evening sitting and, although they were not family, sat together. After explaining the way I work, I began the sitting. Talking to one of the ladies, I asked if she could understand the names David and Richard which I felt could be present-day people. She replied promptly, "Sorry. No." At this, I felt hesitant, as the message came through very positively, so I switched to the second lady, giving evidence of family in spirit and of her present-day happenings. I kept feeling still very unsure of my spirit connections with the first lady, although some older members of her family in spirit which she could accept confirmed details of her house and information about her present-day daughter, but I had a feeling that I was still missing out. Then I was given the surname "Allen" to give to the lady and she replied that this was her own surname. I told her that I was having trouble with someone in spirit who seemed, to me, to be awkward, to which the lady responded that it must be her husband.

As this was being said, I was told he had worn a sort of uniform and I felt surrounded by water and was aware of a very sudden passing. He followed on with the message that he was only in his thirties when he left for the spirit world. To this, his wife stated that he was always "funny" about wearing his uniform, always calling it "a sort of uniform" as it was the merchant navy. Now we had unlocked the spirit confusion, the sitting for this lady got better. He

66

talked of his daughter and the lady's desire to move house but said that she could not at the present time. The gentleman said that he also knew the other lady and joked about their darts team, saying that they often came to watch them play and had to admit that they were both pretty good players. They both laughed and said they had better watch what they said from then on.

I must admit I was still puzzled as I was relating to this spirit person with the surname "Allen" and couldn't understand why no first name, but still hoped it would come through, but before I knew it, the sitting had finished. As I wanted to know, I asked the lady what her husband's first name was. She said, "You know you started with the names of Richard and David? Well, David is my husband and Richard is his brother, but as you said they were present-day, I said 'No' although Richard (his brother) is here". So it was a misunderstanding on both our parts. Basically, spirit had given me the correct names but, because they both came together, and Richard was the last name I had mentioned, I had picked up his presence on earth. I had had to battle with David Allen because I had not been positive at the start and had not stayed and worked at the names given, but David Allen had not given up on us. Although he was annoyed, he persisted and eventually got his messages through. To this, his wife stated she was not going away disappointed and was pleased; she was happy that his life now continues in the spirit world and that his love and help will always be there to guide them in their life here on earth and that he will always be listening in spirit to them.

A Mother's Love

The Spirit world must be a wonderful place,
My beautiful Children are in its embrace.
They passed so suddenly, no time for goodbye,
God knows that I sometimes still need to cry.
I ask Him to keep them safe each night,
I worry so much when they are out of my sight.
My son, baby Julian, I was so proud,
Lorraine, a young lady, I still talk to out loud.
Each day I looked for them, each day I'd search,
Then one day I found them in a Spiritualist Church.
My Children are spirit, God made them free,
It was for a short time, He gave them to me.
My memories are good and still make me smile,
I will see them again, though it seems a long while.
Thanks to the people who help me to cope,
And thanks for God's love, He gave me hope.
My heart has been broken, I feel deep despair,
But one day I'm sure He will answer my prayer.
For Mother's who lost precious Children, like me,
Take heart, they're still with us its just we can't see.
I don't think these words were formed in my head,
They poured from my heart in the tears that I shed.

Written by Carol, Lorraine's Mother.

Lorraine

When someone leaves us for the spirit world, especially if they are very young, they wish to communicate with their loved ones and family, often going to great lengths to make sure a message reaches them. Eventually they are pointed in the direction of the person who will be able to transmit their love and messages, reassuring those left behind that their life now in the spirit world continues, and that they have not forgotten those of us here on the earth plane.

Such was the story of Lorraine, a young lady, who had been in spirit for only a short time. Whenever anyone she knew, or who would have known of her, came for a sitting, Lorraine made her voice known, giving off information about herself and her family in the hope that eventually it would be heard by them and that they would make the journey so that she could talk to them through a medium. This was told me when Carol, Lorraine's mother, visited me for the second time in November, 1991.

Carol had visited me in the previous May with her niece (Lorraine's cousin Anna) and the sitting had been very positive and had brought Carol a lot of peace. Up to then, Carol had been very frustrated as, since Lorraine's sudden passing, she had visited other mediums but got no link with her, nor any message from Lorraine. She had been told that other people got a message from her when they had visited me, so Carol had decided to visit me in hope of getting the communication she needed so badly. No way could I possibly remember that first sitting or recall what had happened, but as the second sitting with Carol and her husband Sam (Lorraine's step-father) was being recorded, I felt it would be nice to use it, with their permission, in the book, as so far the stories in the book had been about young men and this would be a balance.

As it was Sam's first visit, I explained to him, as usual, how I work and what to expect, and the first link I was given was the month of August with a young lady in spirit which was accepted as a passing month. This was followed with the name of Lorraine, saying that she was Carol's daughter. Lorraine said that she was pleased

Lorraine.

that Sam was sitting in with Carol and she could talk to them both. Lorraine confirmed that her passing was sudden and gave the cause of her leaving for the spirit world as a brain haemorrhage, saying she had been just twenty-one. She said that she also had her brother in spirit, who had left many years ago as a baby. She talked to Sam about his self-employment in the building trade, saying it was going on all right and giving the name of one of his work mates, which Sam confirmed. Lorraine also wanted them to know that she had met up with her grandfather, Bill (Carol's dad) whom Lorraine had not known, and also told Sam that she had met his father whom she had known. As there were others with her, Lorraine thought she should mention her young cousins Andrew and Ashley who were with her. She talked about the bungalow the family had lived in, saying they now had a detached house where nothing had really been changed, even her room was as she had had it, mentioning all her fluffy animals still everywhere. At this stage, Lorraine introduced Sue, a friend of Carol's, and Patrick (her boyfriend's) Mum who had now joined her in spirit. She said that Sue had suffered a number of illnesses and had finally taken her life by her own hand and left the earth plane, but wanted to reassure everyone that she was all right and was now at peace with herself, commenting that Carol still saw Sue's daughter, Sally.

Talking once again to Carol, Lorraine laughed about her efforts with the knitting machine and the different problems she had had with the various patterns which Carol was trying to master. Lorraine also thought she should not forget to mention her grandma who was all right and very independent, or Sam's mother whom he saw every day, saying that both of them were reasonably fit.

As some of the present-day families were not seen all that often, Lorraine just mentioned the names of her Aunt Shirley and Uncles Ken and Kevin, and two of Sam's brothers, Michael and Robert. Lorraine felt that she would like to talk to Carol and Sam more about her passing and to reassure them of the decisions that had had to be made, as they both had felt concern as to whether more could have been done. Lorraine asked me to describe the hospital and the life-support machine she had been placed on. She wanted them to know that she had already left for the spirit world when they finally gave permission for it to be switched off. It was the correct decision; nothing more could have been done. To this, Carol and Sam said they had thought maybe it should have been kept on longer but could now accept that it had been done for the best. Lorraine felt she had now reassured those that loved her that they had done everything possible. She was at peace, happy, and with the family members who had met her in spirit.

After the sitting, we talked a little about spiritualism, and Carol explained that, although she had believed in spirit before, she was much more involved since the loss of Lorraine and much more aware. She now visited the Spiritualist church and could not read enough books on the subject, which Carol felt did help her understand a little more.

Lorraine's organs were donated and Carol and Sam said that they were pleased that at least some other families now have a chance of happiness. A young boy had been given Lorraine's heart, someone else can see and at least five people were given a chance to receive help and life, so, although Lorraine had left for the spirit world, others hopefully were now benefiting and their lives could be enhanced. As Carol stated, Lorraine's body was just a shell and her organs no longer any use to her, so why should they be wasted. As Lorraine continues in the world beyond and her spirit with its love and knowledge will be able to come down and show her family not only her love, but guidance, she will watch over them and let them know that she is still listening when they talk to her and not missing out on our lives here on earth.

The Theatre Royal

Since I became spiritually aware in May, 1986, the progression and development of my gift has continued. Hopefully, as each new step and challenge appears, I will have the spiritual strength and physical strength to move on in a positive way. The more you work with spirit, the more aware you become of the directions which they put before you and the opportunities which occur. I saw my gift progress from serving the Spiritualist churches to demonstrations on a slightly larger scale at Women's Institutes and Young Farmers' Clubs and social events at people's houses where there could be anything from twenty-five to two hundred and forty people present. Suddenly, I was approached and asked if I would be interested in taking my gift into theatres to reach a larger audience.

Dawn Perkins and her husband, Geoff, suggested that I should try the Blackfriar's Theatre in Boston, Lincolnshire, a lovely old building that used to be part of a friary. With the help of Monica and Paul, with whom we had all become special friends through the Spiritualist church in Spayne Road, Boston, we organised it. Dawn contacted the theatre and arranged a booking for 31st August, 1991, which left plenty of time for organisation as the date was six months away.

However, in the meantime, I was also approached by Sarah and Christopher who asked whether I would demonstrate at the Theatre Royal at Lincoln if they booked it. I had a little chat with my spirit friend and spiritual partner, Running Foot to see if he felt I was ready for this challenge. He had no hesitation about my accepting, so the commitment was made and the date fixed for 7th June, 1991, which was sooner than the Blackfriars booking and only six weeks ahead.

Afterwards, when I realised that the Theatre Royal seated around five hundred people, I briefly wondered whether I had jumped in at the deep end, but knew that spirit would not have put me in this situation unless I was capable of coping, but only time would prove that. Life continued throughout the following weeks up to the 7th

Blackfriar's Theatre, Boston – 31st August, 1991.

June. Occasionally, during quiet moments, the odd voice or name would appear, which is unusual for me as normally I only get voices when I am working with people. Running Foot, however, confirmed that they would relate on the evening of 7th June, so I said, "Okay, we will see".

The week before this event, I enjoyed a special and lovely experience from spirit. I was contacted by a gentleman called Ken, whom I had met briefly a few months previously, a spiritualist from "way back" who had been out of the movement over the last few years. He 'phoned to ask me if he could drop by for a chat, as he wished to talk about something regarding spirit, so I agreed for Ken to come over one evening following my last sitting. On the Thursday when Ken arrived, I had had a very hectic day and, to be quite honest, could have done without having to see anyone else. However, after a cup of tea, we chatted and Ken asked if we could try some meditation. As this is something I get very little time to do nowadays, and had not meditated with anyone else since the beginning of my spiritual awareness, I proceeded to sit and relax and listen to Ken's voice talking. I could feel myself slowly drifting into a peaceful state, when Ken asked me what I was seeing. I replied that I was being shown a door which was being opened. On being asked what was in the door, I said that all I could see was my guide, Running Foot, who seemed to fill the whole of the door space.

Slowly, Running Foot began to move away from the door and, the next instant, a lady appeared. My first instinctive reaction was, "It cannot be", as I recognised this very famous lady who was a legend in her lifetime while here on the earth plane. There was no way I could possibly have been thinking of her, nor had I heard or seen any news about her in the recent months as she had been in the spirit world for a number of years. However, I remembered her as she was very popular when I was in my twenties and she was not old when she left, rather tragically. What stood out was the way she was dressed; she wore black, fishnet stockings, a black jacket with tails, in her left hand she carried a silver-topped cane and was wearing a top hat on her head, looking just about to do a song and dance. As I looked at her, she just smiled and said, "Yes, it is me" and gave her real name of "Frances Gumm". Of course, we all knew this special lady as "Judy Garland" and I watched as she raised her cane in the air and said, "Right. I will be there to help you on the night. I will give you professional guidance and we will show them!" I could feel myself smiling and wanting to sing, mixed with excitement and the feeling that I wanted to get on with it there and then. Next, with a wave and a big smile, Judy went through the door and was once again replaced by Running Foot who was also smiling.

After explaining my experience to Ken, I was feeling really high. I suddenly realised that spirit had manoeuvred this as if to reassure me that every help would be given to me on this very important step in my spiritual development. I still found it hard to know "Why Judy Garland?" but of course, not only was Judy a truly professional artist, having lead such a traumatic life herself she was a very sensitive being whose whole life had been full of ups and downs that she was now able to come down and help us with our work. I felt very honoured and proud to have been chosen to work with such a special, dedicated professional lady. The next day, I was still "buzzing" and very much aware of Judy's presence but thought I had better keep it quiet, as people would think I had made it up. However, during the week, I did confide in some of my special friends as I felt that they would understand and know that I was not doing so; it was spirit.

Time had passed and it was now just a few days to go to the big night. However much I tried to relate to it, it seemed as if my mind was tuned in to it still being weeks away and not worried. Spirit seemed to have taken control; I had never felt so relaxed. All the sittings were going along positively and, in between them, I would just sit and relax as if I had no cares in the world. I was sleeping well, not even thinking or dreaming and, although it seemed strange, I knew it was right and spirit were getting me prepared. I had arranged to meet Sarah on Friday, 7th June, to visit the theatre and to arrange the stage flowers, and to discuss what I needed on the stage with the very helpful, friendly theatre staff. On stepping on to the empty stage for the first time, I could feel the surge of energy and was very aware of spirit and felt directed to a certain row and seat. I remarked to Sarah, "I already know where the first message will be", as a voice said to me, "My family will be here". Standing on the stage, although the theatre was empty, I already felt at home.

The rest of the day slowly plodded on and, after a light meal and a relaxing bath, it was time to leave for the theatre. The theatre staff were really great and made me feel so much at home. The seats were fully booked and I knew it would be nice and full.

After getting dressed, I felt so relaxed and at ease, it seemed I didn't have a nerve in my body! I was just eager to get out there and get on with the evening. It was now 7.15 pm and time to get in the wings. I said a little prayer and linked up with Running Foot to make sure he was with me and ready to go, and linked with my spirit family and I remember saying to Judy, "Right. It's now or never". The next minute, I was being introduced and I was on stage. It really felt great looking onto the rows of faces and I wasn't really aware of the lights. First, I welcomed everyone and then proceeded to explain what being a medium is and how I hoped the evening would work out. I told the audience that they would themselves have to work as, unless they answered me back, their lovely families in spirit wouldn't be able to get their messages through.

Suddenly, the first spirit voice was there. It was for a young man and it was his uncle speaking and, yes, it was exactly in the spot to which I had been directed earlier in the day. This very positive spirit communicator got the evening off to a very good start, telling his nephew of his passing three years previously from cancer while in his forties, giving his name and passing on advice to his nephew. The rest of the evening flowed along with many messages, some a little sad, but many people's loved ones came through with a great deal of love and lots of laughter, showing that those in the spirit world never change and always want to show their families that life continues.

All too soon, the evening had come to an end, the last message had been passed on and accepted and it was time to chat to those who stayed, answering questions and queries. I also received confirmation that the messages had been understood and many people requested private sittings.

I felt I could have gone back on stage and done it all again. Spirit had shown me that, with their very special love and guidance, I was able to unite with spirit and reach out to those needing help and guidance, no matter how many people were in a place at the time. I had felt very much at home and the challenge had been so easily accepted by spirit; now I felt the honour of being one of spirit's special messengers.

I expected the day following to be a little flat, but in fact the telephone never stopped ringing and callers said how much the messages of the evening had been enjoyed; even people who had not themselves received a message said how much they had enjoyed other people's expressions of surprise over their messages and the laughter that had filled the evening.

Not only is this a very major step on my spiritual ladder, it is wonderful to have an extra special helper from spirit to add to my spiritual family, Judy Garland, who will from now on be with us and give that professional touch and guidance only she would know how. While on the earth plane, Judy brought a lot of joy and pleasure to thousands of people with her marvellous voice and personality, and people felt very drawn to her during the many ups and downs of her short and tragic life. I cannot believe, even now at times, how lucky I am to have been chosen by this very special lady to be spiritually part of her life now.

Since the booking at the Theatre Royal, Lincoln, we have ventured into other theatres, each of which has its own atmosphere, which does help me. Also, the size is important, as a not too large setting is more intimate and the way the stage is set helps the atmosphere.

I am very lucky with my friends who all join in and help, as when we demonstrated at the Blackfriar's Theatre in Boston. Monica beautifully set the stage with flowers and also added a few cats from my collection to add atmosphere which really made me feel at home. Paul organised the music, so relaxing vibrations were making people feel at ease before the show started and during the interval. Dawn did the introductions and kept things flowing, a young lady called Karen handed out flowers for me to people receiving messages and others kindly sold my book, *Just a Touch Away*. This is a title we now use for all our demonstrations as our loved ones are indeed "just a touch away".

I hope that we can continue to show people that spiritualism is nothing to be afraid of and, by spreading it in the theatres, many will have the opportunity of coming into the movement and becoming the mediums and spirit workers of the future.

Having been a spiritually aware person for such a short while and a working medium for even less, I realise my life certainly has changed in many ways, all for the better. The changes have not been only in terms of developing my spiritual gift, but in myself as a person. Now, to me, each day is different – a new experience. Whereas in the past I led rather a routine existence, life has blossomed into a wonderful adventure of seeking and learning new things each day. I meet numerous people who cross my path and enter my life for many different reasons, some never to be seen again, but many who become special friends and helpers and from whom I learn. Being spiritually aware has not only given me an aim in life, but my attitude to people has altered.

In the past, people tried to influence me by impressing their views and opinions on me about both situations and people according to how they saw or felt things should be. Spirit has taught me and helped me, not only to be more open-minded but also to treat everyone as an individual. Now, through my awareness, spirit unravels that person's inner self and shows them as they really are, not perhaps as we see them, nor as they wish to portray themselves to us, but spirit knows that person and can point them in the correct direction with help and guidance to a peaceful existence while here on the earth plane.

My family and friends from the past will recall that I was not a very tolerant person, nor easy at times to live with, but thanks to spirit's love and guidance, things have changed. Where before I would have expressed frustration and anger with people, spirit has taught me to try to understand that person and explore their reasons for being the way they are, not judging until all angles have been explored. In other words, spirit has calmed me down. When I do have something to say, or an opinion to express, they make sure I take time to think it out and hopefully present it in such a way as to respect people's views and feelings.

This was much needed recently when faced with an incident which would, in the past, have "got my back up". On two occasions lately I have been giving a demonstration in local halls. On the first I was helping raise funds for a newly formed ladies' club. It was brought to my notice that, with a certain lady's encouragement, a group of local people were meeting to sing hymns and pray for us on the night of the demonstration. Although I have not met this lady, I am assured that she is a "strong, Christian lady" who does good, and that the group had said they would no longer belong to the ladies' club if the demonstration were allowed to take place. Thankfully, the people who organised my demonstration, decided to judge for themselves and resist the blackmail to control what they could and could not come to see. I am grateful for the time these ladies took to send out their prayers as praying can do no harm, only help to unite us all together.

I thought that would be the end of the matter, but I was wrong.

This month, November, I have again agreed to give a demonstration in the next village to help raise funds at the request of a lady who was at the previous demonstration. Again, these ladies will be holding a hymn and prayer meeting, this time in the local church. It is sad that these Christian people haven't got the courage and decency to actually come to see what my spiritual gift is about and how it works to help those in need, instead of accepting second-hand views and thoughts from others. Whatever good is done, they are unable to accept any other ways of life than their own doctrine. I find, with all this, I can smile and not get worked up, but to try and understand their narrow outlook. I ask spirit to pray for them that one day they will at least be able to accept that people have freedom of choice; that, just because something does not agree with their belief system, that is no reason to stop others from finding what could be their pathway in life to bring them happiness and peace. After this month's demonstration, I shall write to thank this lady and her friends for their concern and prayers. Even within our own Spiritualist churches, there are those who wish to dictate and say who should and who should not be part of spiritual gatherings, as was brought home to me by my guide, Running Foot.

In July, 1990, for some unknown reason, I was being made aware of my right forearm and the image of having a tattoo of Running Foot placed upon it. All my life, I had never wanted a tattoo, so at my age I could not understand why I should want one now. I mentioned this to my sister, Jenny, saying I could not understand it, as the thought was so strong. I said I thought I just wanted someone to convince me I was just imagining it. This went on for six weeks until one afternoon when I was not working, I made my way to Lincoln where there was the only tattooist I knew. After walking by the building a few times and convincing myself that I was not being influenced by my own thoughts, I went in and explained what I wanted. The next minute, I was sitting down and the work had begun. On walking out, I honestly didn't know how I felt. I suppose my own thoughts came through and I just tried to think of how I was going to explain this mad burst of youth to my family and friends. I need not have worried. Most people thought it was a great idea. Even my mother only passed an indifferent remark about it and didn't query "why".

It was only after this had happened that I understood why Running Foot had wanted me to have a tattoo, because of the attitude of many people mostly of the older generation who would "Tut", and remark on the younger people who visited churches with tattoos on view, as if, because of their appearance, they were not welcome in the church. It is as if tattooed people are an element or type of person who should not be encouraged to participate in spiritualism. However, now I myself, as a platform medium, can stand up and give the service showing my tattoo, showing that whatever we are or the way we like to look, what is important is the person and what is within. I feel spirit will always try to make the point to the people that everyone is welcome whatever race, creed, or station in life they hold, that appearances are not always important and we should not just judge on what we see, but search for what is within.

Paul
(continued from Just a Touch Away)

Those who have read, *Just a Touch Away*, will, I am sure, remember the story of young Paul (Lucy's son) who left us for the spirit world in November, 1989 and the poems Lucy wrote in his memory. This month was the anniversary of Paul's second year in the spirit world and Lucy had arranged for the family to come for a sitting. It was rather a foggy day when Lucy arrived with Paul's sister, Sam, and Daniel, his brother. Also with them were Paul's grandmother and his aunt and uncle, Sandra and Tony. They had battled with the weather all the way from Brighton and were a little weary.

Paul came through as usual with his love and wanted to let them know he had been watching what they had all been up to since he last spoke to them ten months previously. First, Paul wanted to congratulate Daniel on passing his driving test. He told Daniel that he should now learn mechanics so that he would know what was under the bonnet of the car. He also wanted to say to Sam that he was very happy about the baby and letting her know of the date when it would be due in January, 1992, saying that he would be there at the birth. We then talked to his grandmother and talked about her health, joking about how he was with her when she sat with her feet in the bowl giving them a good soak, and that he was sending her healing down for her feet, which made his grandmother smile. This was the first visit for Paul's Aunty Sandra (and Uncle Tony, and Paul then decided to talk to them. He said that he knew that they now had an aviary and remarked on the finches that had bred. He also talked of their three children, especially young "Jo" (Joanne) their daughter, saying that lately she had become rather cheeky, and that she had just had her hair cut short (this was confirmed as having happened the day before) and mentioned his uncle's work in the building trade. He talked about the jobs which needed doing at home – the draughty front door and especially the wall which needed attention in the back yard. All this was accepted. Paul wanted to give special love to his mum, Lucy, and Dave – his stepdad – and the rest of his brothers and sister.

Paul wanted to talk of his mum's special work which he was helping with and this is one of the reasons I felt that I should like to include Paul in *I'm Here Listening*, hoping that it will show people that out of sadness and loss, even of someone so young and special, good can come. Our loved ones in spirit can help us here on the earth plane and, through someone close to them, can guide and point in the correct direction, as Paul has done with Lucy. Although Lucy has not only her husband, Dave, but also five children at home to look after, she now works to help others who have lost loved ones. Now, not only belonging to the local Boston Support Group, Lucy finds herself travelling and working in conjunction with the East Sussex Police, being at hand to give counselling (for which she attended a course) and giving talks to many groups including police recruits, on helping and liaising with families who have sadly lost someone suddenly, perhaps in a very difficult situation. Therefore, support and comfort is on hand at this crucial time as so many have difficulty coming to terms, with their loss and may have no-one to turn to for help and advice. Although, at times, Lucy finds this frustrating and time-consuming she bravely battles on with the challenge, knowing that Paul there beside her and, with Paul, Lucy can now help others and strengthen their bond together, working with spirit.

To me, Lucy is one of those very special people who has a lot of love and support from her family. I feel very privileged and lucky to know her and her family. I know that now I can put those who come to see me into the safe hands of Lucy, knowing that they will be given the best possible help and guidance.

On Lucy's visit to me, I was presented with a special present Lucy had made for me. It was a knitted doll in the form of Running Foot, my friend and guide, with the apologies that she had unfortunately been unable to give him a head-dress as there were no feathers from the chickens that would have been suitable. This is typical of the person Lucy is.

Once more, I am including two poems which Lucy sent me a while ago which I hope will help to comfort each and every one of you.

still here.

23-9-90.

Each of us is gwen a day and time to die.

for whatever reason some cannot say good bye.

Some are old, and many young, still strolling down lifes way.

Each is given love and joy, on their special day.

Broken hearts and grief untold, for those who still remain.

loose not heart, nor cry to long, for all is still the same

The love you shared still goes on, growing all the time.

Ever watchfull, close by, one day you'll see a sign.

Perhaps a fleeting glimpse, or whisper in the air.

for they never leave you, forever they are there.

"windrush"
0205-84-343.
2-10-90.

Dear Bryan, I hope my letter, short as
it may be, finds you well. You're
truly my inspiration, 10 mins after
talking to you I put pen to paper
the results are enclosed. I just hope
I can return the compliment, and
inspire you!!. The other poem's I
wrote earlier (last month). I asked
Paul to help me with the seconds
one, "Talk to Me", so its a joint
effort! I do hope you don't mind
me sending them to you, but you
never know, they may perhaps help
some one one day. Well I must close
now, keep in touch.
                    Love Lucy x

Talk to Me.

Am I talking to myself, no of course
I'm not.

I'm talking to my son, I ask his help a
lot.

My conversation seems one sided, and
odd to those around.

But the answers to my problems with
his help are found.

I say Good night, God Bless, Son, when
I go to bed.

He listens very carefully to all that
I have said

I know I cannot see him, nor his
closeness can I touch.

But I know my conversations, to
him, mean so very much.

Adrian And Keith
(Known as Ted)

For us to lose a member of the family is very hard to come to terms with and accept whatever age they may be, but for a family to have two young people leave for the spirit world suddenly and within the space of two months is very difficult indeed to accept or to avoid wondering why life can be so harsh.

My first encounter with these two very special brothers called Adrian and Keith (known to his friends as Ted) was in the month of June, 1991, when a young lady called Lorraine visited me for a sitting. During the course of the sitting, information came through about her boyfriend Ted and the plans they were hoping to carry out. I was being made aware of a close spirit connection with Ted. I related to Lorraine that Ted had brothers, one of whom had left very recently for the spirit world and that, although Lorraine did not know him personally, she knew of him through Ted. Lorraine said that this was correct and Ted's brother then related more details about himself, saying that he wore a Navy uniform and that his passing had not been through illness but had been of his own choice. Lorraine answered that she could accept this but, as it had just recently happened (during May), she was unsure of the exact details. Ted and his family had been told only recently and information was still being put together. To this the spirit voice followed on by giving his name as Adrian and spoke of his wife and the daughters he had left behind. Adrian hoped that Lorraine would be able to tell his mother and family that he was now at peace with himself and was free from his problems, as Adrian said that he knew it would be very hard for his family to accept or understand why he left in the way he had.

Because of his work and the fact that his family lived on the south coast, they did not know anything of his life apart from when he came home on visits. As the sitting finished, Lorraine said that she would pass on the messages to Adrian's family and would try to get Ted to see me, as Adrian had spoken during the sitting of wanting to talk to him.

Adrian.

Keith (Ted).

It was the following month, July, when I saw Lorraine again. She arrived unexpectedly in a very distressed and emotional state, asking if I could spare her a few moments. Of course, I did not hesitate.

As Lorraine sat down, my first words to her were, "It's about Ted isn't it?" and Lorraine nodded. The next message I got was to say to Lorraine that Ted wanted to say he was all right. He had met up with his brother and wanted to send his love to Lorraine.

Obviously, it was very difficult for Lorraine, as while all this information was being relayed to her, she was very emotionally affected and naturally some of it was difficult to absorb straight away, but she wanted to continue. Ted, therefore, went on to give her further evidence about the hospital, stating that they placed him on a life-support machine but wanted her to know that he had already left at that point and was united with his, brother, Adrian. All this had happened as the result of an accident between his motor bike and a car but that, as it had all happened so quickly, he had not suffered. He said the accident had happened two days ago while he was working further south. Lorraine tearfully confirmed all this, saying the accident had happened near Oxford. She said, "Tell Ted I love him", to which came back the reply, "I know. Tell Lorraine I love her too". A little while after this short sitting, Lorraine thanked me and asked if she could come back again at a later date.

In the August, Lorraine once again came to see me, this time bringing along someone called Jean, who as the sitting progressed, proved to be Ted's sister. He gave her a little telling off and talked about her work, in general pulling her leg a bit, talking to her about how he was and saying that Adrian was joining in with the messages. Both Jean and Lorraine seemed pleased with their linking up with the boys and said they were going to take the tape for their mother to hear.

It was October when I next had contact with Adrian and Ted. This time a lady had arranged to have a sitting and, I believe, gave her name as "Peggy". As the sitting began, I was made aware of her parents in spirit, giving information about themselves and then suddenly I was made very much aware of Adrian, with his uniform. As I relayed the information to this lady, I suddenly realised who I was now talking to. It was the boys' mum and then they gave me another name, which she said was her real name.

Firstly, Adrian wanted to talk with his mother to explain about his passing, stating the way in which he left for the spirit world, giving details of how he passed and saying that he was just into his thirties. Adrian continued to try to explain his reasons for making such a decision, saying that it had been planned. He knew it would be difficult for his mother to understand because, as he lived away from home with his wife and daughters, his mother would have been unaware of his life and its problems. To Adrian, the Navy had always been his one love and this always had priority in whatever he aimed for. His mother agreed. Adrian tried his best to explain and to reassure her that, at the time of his passing, he had felt it was to him the right decision. Now he was at peace with himself and was there to meet his brother, Keith (Ted) when he had arrived so quickly in spirit. Adrian also wanted to mention his father and sisters and his brother, Julian. He talked a little of his wife and children and knew they would be looked after. By this time, Keith was getting impatient as he wanted to talk to his mother about his own passing. He was only in his late twenties and wanted to talk to his mother about the decisions they had had to make in switching off the life-support machine reassuring them that it had been the correct thing to do, as he held already been in the spirit world, having joined up with Adrian and his grandparents. Keith talked about Lorraine, his girlfriend, saying that they had not been engaged for long, but that she was now close to the family and helping them all. Keith then talked seriously about his terraced house which, he knew, was going to be sold. He was rather concerned as he had not made a will. He wanted his mother to benefit from it but knew there might be a problem, which his mother confirmed. His natural parents had divorced and his father had moved to South Africa quite a while before. His mother had talked of having to let him know about everything, but Keith did not want him to have a claim on anything. Keith hoped that everything would be done as he wished and his mother said she would do her best. Thy continued to talk about other things and then Keith wanted her to know how pleased he was that so many came to say, "Goodbye", commenting about all the bikers from the motor bike club to which he and Lorraine belonged, giving off some of their names which his mother was able to accept.

Both Adrian and Keith continued to give more messages to their mother, especially about the family, commenting on father's bowling and saying they would now be watching and trying to help. The sitting had been completely recorded so that, once again, the family could all listen to it.

Marilyn. Photo from Keith's (Ted's) home.

After the sitting, we chatted generally, and Adrian's mother gave me a photograph of him in his uniform to add to my collection, as I already had one of Keith (Ted) which Lorraine had dropped in for me. About a week later, I received a phone call from the boys' mother asking if I would like a picture of Marilyn Monroe which had belonged to Keith, as they were emptying his house and had thought of me, because of the many pictures I have around my house of Marilyn and that it would add to the collection. I was delighted to accept and they promised to bring it over the following week. When it did arrive, it was beautiful and now has a very prominent place in the front room for all to see. Keith's mother said that there is a matching one of James Dean by the same artist and in an identical frame and offered me that also. It, too, is now hanging on the wall in the hallway. These pictures are now very special to me and will always be a close link with Keith and his family.

Since then, Julian, their older brother, has also paid me a visit and both Adrian and Keith came and talked to him, giving information about his family and his work. They understood that Julian was a little unsure whether he should come for a sitting but were pleased that he did and soon gave him answers to his thoughts and reassurance about his family and life in general. Now, nearly all the family have heard in their own time from the brothers and know that they are in the spirit world together, at peace with themselves.

The family knows that Adrian and Keith will be listening to everyone. When love and messages are sent out to them, they are received as they are by all of our loved ones, and love and strength is sent in return to us here on the earth plane, to help us to continue with our lives, hopefully in peace, love and harmony.

Still Plateau

Still plateau on the edge of the world,
Sit gazing at the endless swirls.
Of light in time, apeace to heart,
The love of life,
Still waters part.

A stillness dreamt or witnessed raw,
Absorb the gift of love, a pure and
Simple thing that needs no sound,
A rainbows radiance,
Sometimes found.

August, 1988. From a poem by Martin Sargent.